Rising Above the Crowd

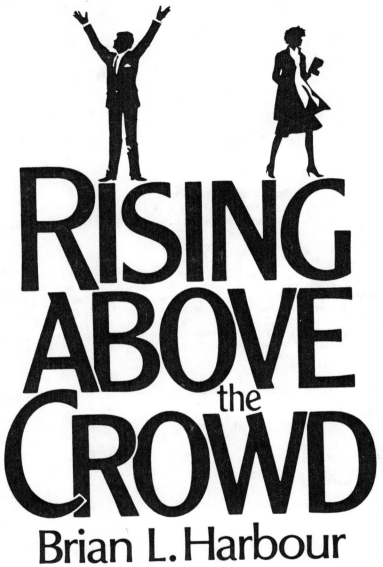

RISING ABOVE the CROWD

Brian L. Harbour

BROADMAN PRESS
Nashville, Tennessee

© Copyright 1988 • Broadman Press
All rights reserved
4257-30
ISBN: 0-8054-5730-5

Dewey Decimal Classification: 248.4
Subject Heading: CHRISTIAN LIFE
Library of Congress Catalog Card Number: 87-17361

Printed in the United States of America

Library of Congress Cataloging-in-Publication Data

Harbour, Brian L.
    Rising above the crowd / Brian L. Harbour.
    p. cm.

    ISBN 0-8054-5730-5
    1. Christian life.   2. Success.   I. Title
BV4501.2.H339 1988   87-17361
248.4'861—dc19   CIP

Dedicated to
my spiritual family
at
Immanuel Baptist Church
in
Little Rock, Arkansas
who demonstrate excellence as a people of God
and
motivate me to be the best I can be.

Contents

1
Living Beneath Your Privileges

Herman and Henrietta were touring their brand-new house, a house that Henrietta had paid for with her money, a fact of which she often reminded Herman. In each room of the house, she said to her husband, "Herman, if it were not for my money, we wouldn't be here." Herman didn't say a word.

That afternoon a truck delivered to the house a load of furniture, furniture which Henrietta paid for with her money. After the furniture was in place, the couple toured the house again. As they observed each room, beautifully appointed and magnificently decorated, Henrietta reminded her husband, "Herman, if it were not for my money, this furniture would not be here." Again, Herman was silent.

Late in the afternoon a truck came with a special piece of furniture which was to be the focal point of the den, a combination stereo-television-computer all wrapped into one gorgeous piece of furniture which Henrietta paid for with her money. When it was in place, Henrietta again addressed her beleaguered husband, "If it were not for my money, that piece of furniture would not be here." Finally, Herman spoke, "Honey, I don't want to make you feel bad, but if it were not for your money, I wouldn't be here!"

Why are you here? Have you ever asked yourself that question? Have you ever considered the fact that you are on this earth to accomplish something with your life?

Five billion people live in our world. Most of these people move silently from the womb to the tomb without making even a ripple on the sea of life. Others stir the waters around them and eventually rise above the crowd. Surrounded by people who muddle along in mediocrity, these special individuals move toward excellence. They make a mark.

Why?

I wanted to know the answer to that question because I believe we are here for a reason, not merely to exist but to exert a positive influence on life. God has planted a certain potential within each one of us, and we need to realize that potential. Rather than settling down into mediocrity, we need to be willing to move toward excellence.

So how does one rise above the crowd? Some basic and simple principles mark the difference between those mired in mediocrity and those who achieve excellence. These principles are for everybody and for every age. No circumstance in your life can keep you from learning these principles and growing through them. These principles will not enable you to do everything you want to do. However, they will enable you to do better what you can do. These principles will enable you to achieve excellence in life.

What Is Success?

Success is a popular subject today. What is success? Three men were discussing that question one day. One of the men commented, "I'll tell you what success is. Success means that you achieve something so significant that you are invited by the president for a personal conference in the White House. That's success."

"No," interrupted the second man, "I'll tell you what success is. Success means that you achieve something significant and are invited for a private conference with the president. Then, as you talk, the red emergency phone rings. However, the president is so engrossed in his conversation with you that he refuses to answer the phone. That's success."

The third man retorted, "You're both wrong. I'll tell you what success is. Success means you achieve something significant in life; you are invited for a private conference with the president. As you talk, the red emergency phone rings. The president does answer it. After a moment he holds the phone out and says, 'Here, it's for you.' That's success!"

Success usually brings to mind financial achievement or being number one. This is not a book about success. It is a book about excellence. There is a difference between the two. Success means being *the* best. Excellence means being *your* best. Success, to many, means being better than everyone else. Excellence means being better tomorrow than you were yesterday. Success means exceeding the achievements of other people. Excellence means matching your practice with your potential.

Not *the* Best but *your* Best

Excellence does not mean being *the* best. Excellence means being *your* best. Understanding that difference makes all the difference in the world.

Only one team wins the Super Bowl in professional football each year. Yet, many teams can achieve excellence in their seasons if they match their practice with their potential. The World Series in baseball ends with only one team the champion. Yet many teams can achieve excellence in their seasons if they become the best team they can be with the resources and talent they have.

Often we look at ourselves in the mirror with condemnation and say, "You're not as good looking as Betty Beautiful. You're not as suave as Sam Smooth." That is the wrong measure by which to judge ourselves.

Excellence is not to be measured by the potential of others or by their achievements. It is measured by your potential. The true measure is not outward but inward. Match your practice with your potential and you will achieve excellence. Be *your* best and you will experience excellence.

Not Winning by Intimidation

Neither is excellence achieved at the expense of others. The principles in this book have nothing to do with intimidation or manipulation. Excellence achieved at the expense of others is not true excellence. Rising above the crowd does not demand that you push others under the feet of the crowd. Rising above the crowd means that you realize your potential, that you develop yourself into the best you that you can possibly be.

What keeps us from rising above the crowd is not the success of others. Rather, the culprit is our willingness to live beneath our privileges.

Living Beneath Your Privileges

You may have read the story of Bertha Adams. She was a pitiful case. She was seventy-one years old and weighed only fifty pounds. She begged door-to-door for food and clothed her emaciated body with Salvation Army clothing. On April 5, 1974, she died of malnutrition in West Palm Beach after spending the last few days of her life in the nursing home. When Bertha died, authorities discovered that she left behind a fortune of over one million dollars, including more than $800,000 in cash and several hundred shares of valuable stock which she had stored in two safety deposit boxes. She was rich, but she lived in poverty.[1]

That is more than the tragic tale of one woman. It is the story of literally thousands of men and women who have abundant resources and yet live their lives in emotional and spiritual poverty.

If you are satisfied with what you are and where you are, you will not be interested in this book. On the other hand, if you are tired of wasting your life, if you are tired of living beneath your privileges, if you are tired of being mired in mediocrity, then this book is for you. Across on page 11 are the principles which can help you achieve excellence and thus rise above the crowd.

1. Decide where you want to go.
2. Avoid the side streets.
3. Learn how to see things as they can be.
4. Act now.
5. Develop good habits.
6. Refuse to give up.
7. Keep learning.
8. Be a giver.
9. Learn to move past your failures.
10. Bring God into the situation through prayer.
11. Remember that life is a team sport.

2
When You Get Where You're Going, Will You Be There?

A family began a vacation to a destination which would take several days of driving to reach. As they hit the road for the third day of their trip, the eight-year-old daughter, weary from the traveling, asked: "Daddy, when we get where we're going, will we be there?"

That is an important question to ask about your life. No single factor so determines the quality of your life as the goals you set for yourself. Where do you want to go? What do you want to do with your life? What is your desired destination?

A study of two hundred life histories of outstanding people revealed that they had ordered lives which were steered toward selected goals. Each person had something to live for. Another study of individuals who committed suicide indicated that they felt their lives had become intolerable because they had nothing to aim for, no goal to seek. In each case, goals, or lack of them, were the difference.[1]

We often talk about discovering who we are. The truth is we do not discover who we are. We decide who we are. And that decision is made in the goals we set for our lives.

How do you achieve excellence? The first principle is:

DECIDE WHERE YOU WANT TO GO

I Want That Mountain

Do you know Caleb? He's not as famous as Abraham or Moses or some other biblical personalities. Yet, he's one of my favorite characters because he knew what he wanted in life.

Two brief glimpses are given of Caleb. The first cameo pictures him as one of the twelve spies sent by Moses to bring back a report on Canaan, the land God told the Hebrews to possess. When the twelve returned, ten of them said, "There is no way we can take possession of the land. The people are too big. The cities are too strong. The challenge is too great. And we are too small and insignificant. There is no way we can do it." Two of the spies disagreed. Their minority opinion was, "Let us go up at once and possess the land, for we are well able to do it."[2] One of those two was Caleb. Caleb had a dream that focused on the land God promised the Hebrews. And he was ready to act upon his conviction.

The next cameo of Caleb pictures him forty-five years later. The doubting Hebrews were forced to wander in the wilderness for forty years. Finally, all the doubters died, and God was ready to start again with a new generation. This time the Hebrews moved in obedience to God and established a foothold in their Promised Land. This is when Caleb appears again. God had specifically promised him the land of Hebron. Now, at eighty-five years of age, he was ready to make his claim. Approaching Joshua, Caleb declared, "That is the mountain God promised to me, and now, I want that mountain."[3]

There are three ages of mankind: youth, middle age, and, "My, but you're looking well!" Caleb was in that third group, and holding. Yet, he knew where he wanted to go. He was a man with a plan.

Never Too Old

Caleb was eighty-five years old when he declared, "I want that mountain!" Eighty-five is the time most people think about sitting back and settling in. Not Caleb. After a lifetime of faithful service to others, Caleb set his eyes on Hebron and asserted, "I want that mountain."

Caleb is in a parade of men and women who have made great accomplishments in the later stages of their lives. Consider this senior citizen hall of heroes. Goethe at eighty completed *Faust.* Tennyson at eighty-three wrote "Crossing the Bar." Michelangelo completed his greatest work of art at the age of eighty-seven. Justice Oliver Wendell Holmes set down some of his most brilliant legal opinions at age ninety. Albert Schweitzer still headed his hospital in Africa at the age of eighty-nine. When he was eighty-eight, Konrad Adenauer was chancellor of Germany. Winston Churchill wrote his four-volume work, *A History of the English Speaking People,* when he was eighty-two.

You are never too old to set goals.

It Won't Be Easy

An automobile salesman drove a brand-new demonstrator home, a sporty convertible. His wife persuaded him to let her drive it to the supermarket. She returned in a few minutes, red faced and flustered. "Every truck driver I met honked his horn and waved at me," she complained. "Guys on the sidewalk were whistling at me. I don't know what's going on." Her husband took her outside and showed her the promotional sign attached to the back of the car. The sign read, "I don't cost as much as you think."

Don't hang that sign on your goals. They do cost. Goals are not instantaneously achieved, nor are they easily reached. For Caleb to claim his mountain he had to run the giants out of the land. As you strive to reach your goals, as you attempt to claim your mountain, you too will have to overcome some giants.

The giant of *adversity* will have to be faced. You will never attempt anything significant in life without someone trying to stop you. Opponents will stand in your way. Some will criticize; many will discourage you.

I visited a church in Waco, Texas, as a young minister to determine if I would become their pastor. After I preached, the church voted on whether to call me. Three people voted against me! Actually, just one person was against me, but she told her husband and son how to vote. Three votes against me! I never did discover why she didn't like me. Maybe my hair was too long. Or she might not have liked my clothes. Maybe she did not like the fact that I was so young. For some reason, she did not like me. She appointed herself a committee of one to make life miserable for me. But do you know what happened? We simply went around her. We decided it was her problem and not ours. We refused to allow her opposition to stop what God called us to do.

Adversity will rise before you in any task you attempt. You can count on it. Walt Disney understood that. In fact, rumor has it that whenever he had a new idea, he would ask ten people what they thought of it. If they were unanimous in their rejection of the idea, he would begin to work on it immediately. Walt Disney overcame adversity on his way to excellence.[4]

The giant of *laziness* will need to be dealt with. The reason so many muddle along in mediocrity is that they are too lazy to do anything. Not lack of opportunity, not lack of ability, but lack of desire is at times our worst adversary.

A certain housewife answered the doorbell one morning to greet a door-to-door salesman. He told her he had a labor-saving device that would cut her housework in half. She told him she wanted two of them! Some people are like that all of the time. All people are like that some of the time. The easiest thing to do is to do nothing. That human tendency, to do just as little as we can, will have to be faced and overcome. Excellence comes to those who move out of the passive voice into the active.

The giant of *envy* will have to be overcome. As we see others accomplishing great things, we can easily allow the green-eyed monster called envy to take possession of our minds and dissipate our energies and distract us from our own goals.

A classic case of envy was highlighted in the movie *Amadeus.* Amadeus Mozart crushed the dreams of Antonio Salieri during the eighteenth century. Salieri desired to make a significant contribution to the world of music. The problem was that Salieri created music in the same way that he lived: carefully, plodding, by the rule book, but without color, passion, or high inspiration. Salieri's desire was channeled into a life of devotion to God which he hoped God would reward with the ability to produce glorious music. Despite his desire and devotion, Salieri's music lacked life.

Mozart, on the other hand, was presented as an arrogant, giggling, undisciplined, foul-mouthed, sexually promiscuous upstart. Angry at God for choosing to give Mozart the ability to write some of the most exquisite music ever heard on earth, Salieri then directed his anger at Mozart. Anger eventually became vengefulness. Consequently, the talent Salieri did have was dissipated in his blinding envy toward Mozart. Salieri desired to destroy Mozart. In the end, he also destroyed himself.

Like the monsters of old movies which, after being created, turned on their creators, so envy conceived in the heart then becomes a raging monster that eventually destroys its creator. These giants and more will block your path as you reach for your goals.

From Jail to Yale

Charles Dutton was born in Baltimore. Raised in a housing project with parents who divorced when he was three, Charles found his acceptance and satisfaction on the streets where the tough, older guys became his heroes. He quit school in the eighth grade and spent his time with his street friends. His life hit rock bottom at the age of seventeen. In a fight with a neighborhood kid, Charles pulled a knife and stabbed him. Consequently, he was sentenced to eighteen months in prison. Paroled after seven months, he was soon back in prison again. This time the sentence was three years.

Dutton's penchant for fighting and trouble followed him into prison. Nearing the end of his term, Charles instigated a prison riot. Eight more years were tacked onto his sentence.

Charles did not participate in any of the prison activities. His only outlet was reading. This door eventually put him on the pathway toward a new life. He decided one day to read a play, *Day of Absence*, by Douglas Turner Ward. When he persuaded some inmates to join him in putting on the play, something happened. "I knew right away," he said, "that this was what I had been meant to do." He continued, "I wanted to act more than I had ever wanted anything else in my life."

How does a twenty-two-year-old man, without a high school diploma, with an unfinished prison term, realize his dream to become an actor? It wasn't easy. He began by earning a high-school-equivalency diploma. His progress convinced the parole board to release him in 1976. This enabled him to enroll in Towson State University in Maryland to study acting. Through the passion of his dream and the uniqueness of his skill, Charles impressed the chairman of the department. He encouraged Charles to apply for a scholarship at the Yale Drama School, which he was awarded in 1982. At the age of thirty-four, Charles was on Broadway playing the role of a black trumpet player in *Ma Rainey's Black Bottom.* Based on that play, the *New York Times* referred to him as "one of the season's most talked-about actors."

"From jail to Yale," and even beyond that, is the story of Charles Dutton, a young man who was lifted from the depths of shame to the threshold of excellence because he had a dream. He made his dream, and then his dream made him.[5]

Where Do You Start?

So where do you start in setting the goals for your life? The first step is a careful analysis of yourself, your gifts, your interests, and of the things that excite you. God created you with unique gifts and a distinct destiny. Since excellence comes in matching your practice with the potential God placed within you, the first step is to assess your potential accurately.

When a certain man died, he was elated that heaven sported some of the most beautiful golf courses he had ever seen. He was enjoying the layout of one course when he saw a golfer approach the tee, set the ball down, and then attempt to drive the ball four hundred yards over a clump of trees. He overheard one of the crowd say to another, "Who does he think he is, Saint Peter?" The response, "He *is* Saint Peter. Trouble is, he thinks he's Jack Nicklaus."

You can go through life trying to be someone else if you want to. It is your life and your choice. Excellence comes, however, when you set your goals on the realization of the potential God has planted within you.

How Do You Eat an Elephant?

"I'm so hungry I could eat an elephant," the little boy said to his dad. Since the child was prone to exaggeration, the father pressed him on his statement. "How could you eat an elephant?" the father queried. In a flash, the boy responded, "One bite at a time."

How do you reach your goals? One step at a time. In other words, long-term goals have to be supplemented with short-term goals which will provide progress toward the long-range goals. After you determine where you want to be two years from now, determine what you have to do today and tomorrow and next week to arrive at that eventual destination.

Two men were walking in the woods one day when they saw a huge black bear coming toward them. One of the men quickly put on his jogging shoes. The other man said, "You can't outrun that big bear." The man putting on his shoes responded, "I don't have to outrun that bear. I just have to outrun you."

One must have the proper perspective, focus his attention on the immediate goal at hand, cut to the heart of the issue, determine what needs to be done, and commit himself to the achievement of that immediate goal.

One Fatal Flaw

Your goals need to cover every area of your life. To set business goals but not family goals is insufficient. To achieve spiritually but fail physically will prevent you from knowing true excellence. Excellence comes through a balance of achievement in every area of life.

A college basketball coach was confronted with the latest

grades of his star player. He made four *F's* and one *D*. "What do you have to say about that?" the dean asked the coach. The coach responded, "I think he's been concentrating too much on one subject." Concentrating too much on one subject to the neglect of others will not lead to excellence but to tragedy.

Friedrich Flick, West German industrialist, achieved a level of success that few people attain. When he died, he left a personal fortune of $1.5 billion and a business empire that embraced all or part of some three hundred firms. At his death, his empire generated annual sales in excess of $3 billion. The *Newsweek* article announcing Flick's death concluded with this evaluation: "But for all his enormous power and wealth, the old man had one very human shortcoming: he could not control his family."[6]

Friedrich Flick was successful according to the standards of the world. He did not experience excellence, however, for excellence comes in a balanced life of achievement.

Am I Making Progress?

Is your goal specific enough for you to know whether or not you have achieved it? That is an important question. The reason many of us do not achieve our goals is that they are not measurable. Therefore, we never really know if we reach them.

Compare, for instance, these two goals: (1) My goal is to expand my mind, or (2) My goal is to read forty books this year. Which goal is measurable?

Compare these two goals: (1) I want to get in better shape physically, or (2) I want to lose twenty-five pounds.

Goals that cannot be measured will not motivate.

Not only must the goals be measurable. You must periodically check your progress. Suppose your goal is to lose twenty-five pounds in six months. If, at the end of three months, you have not lost any weight, this is a signal that you need to change your strategy.

The goal-setting pattern is followed by successful athletes. They are constantly taking inventory of their lives, finding their weaknesses and correcting them, discovering their strengths and developing them.

Anyone can set goals. Developing the strategy to reach those goals, then periodically evaluating your progress and making the proper mid-course corrections is what makes the difference between mediocrity and excellence.

When You Can't See the Land

The year was 1952. The scene was the California coast. It was the Fourth of July. Florence Chadwick, aged thirty-four, waded into the water off Catalina Island and began her twenty-one mile swim toward California. If she completed the challenge, she would be the first woman ever to swim from Catalina to California.

The water was ice cold, and the fog was so heavy Florence could hardly see the boats in her own party. Sharks often came close and had to be driven off with rifles. The numbing cold of the water was her severest problem.

Fifteen hours later, numbed with the cold, she asked to be taken out. She couldn't go on. Her mother and trainer, alongside in the boat, told her they were near land. They encouraged her not to quit. But as she looked ahead, all she could see was the dense fog. She wanted to get out. When they pulled her out of the water, she was only a half mile from the California coast!

Later, when Florence's body began to thaw, the shock of failure finally hit her. To a reporter she blurted out, "Look, I'm not excusing myself. But if I could have *seen* the land, I might have made it."[7]

The waters of life often chill us to the bone, and our arms are weary with the struggle. We want to get out. But if we can just lift up our eyes and *see* the goal ahead of us, we will make it.

Points to Remember

When you get where you are going on the road that you are now traveling—with your habits, your relationships, your daily activities, and your attitudes—will you be where you want to be? If not, decide to do something about it now.

Remember:

1. It is never too late or too early to begin.
2. Reaching your goals will not be easy.
3. Evaluate yourself to determine your gifts, your potential, and your desires.
4. Decide on your long-range goal, your ultimate purpose for living. Then determine the daily and weekly goals that will help you reach that ultimate destination.
5. Set goals which will motivate you to progress in every area of life—socially, spiritually, physically, financially, personally, professionally, and in your family life.
6. Establish regular times of evaluation when you measure your progress.

Excellence comes to those who know where they want to go.

3
Are You Chasing Stags
Or Watching Mouse Holes?

The story is told of a bloodhound which started a hunt chasing a stag. A fox crossed the path, so the hound chased the fox. After a while a rabbit crossed the path, so the hound chased it. Later, a mouse crossed the path, and the hound chased the mouse into the hole. The hound began his hunt on the trial of a magnificent stag, and he ended up watching a mouse hole!

That is a parable of the life of many today. They establish their goals, they decide where they want to go, they set out after some magnificent stag, but then they are diverted onto a side street, and they end up watching a mousehole.

So here is the second principle which will enable you to achieve excellence:

> AVOID THE SIDE STREETS

A Hero from the Past

Perhaps the greatest hero of the Hebrew people was Joseph. What a man he was! He was one about whom the Hebrew mothers would tell their sons; Joseph was the kind of husband they wanted for their daughters. What was so special about Joseph? He learned some important lessons in the Graduate School of Hard Knocks. He was the favored son of the Hebrew patriarch, Jacob. His brothers hated him because his father loved him so. Consequently, Joseph's brothers sold him as a slave, hoping to get rid of him. He weathered the storms of his life in Egypt and eventually became a leader of Egypt, providing the resources which enabled his brothers to survive a famine in their own land. In these dramatic experiences, Joseph learned three lessons that helped him achieve excellence.

First, *Joseph learned how to say "whoa."* Genesis 37 relates one of the most remarkable personal turnabouts in all the Bible. We speak often of the rise "from rags to riches." Joseph was involved in a descent from riches to rags. This was the "American dream" in reverse. Chapter 37 begins with a description of Joseph as the "fair-haired" son of a wealthy patriarch who was honored as his father's favorite son. The chapter ends with Joseph en route to Egypt as a slave.

In Egypt, Joseph rose above his circumstances, advancing to a position of importance in Potiphar's household. Just when Joseph thought he had it made, Potiphar's wife conspired against him, and once more he was in chains, this time in an Egyptian prison.

Joseph was confronted by problem after problem. Suffering and trouble were his constant companions. However, he refused to let trouble divert him onto the side road of despair. When trouble came, Joseph learned how to say whoa. He patiently preservered until he could transform his adversity into opportunity.

Joseph then learned a second lesson. He learned how to say "no." In the midst of his troubles, another side road opened before him, a pathway labeled "temptation." Joseph was a handsome young man. Potiphar's wife became infatuated with him. When the opportunity arose, she approached Joseph with this suggestion: "Let's go to bed together."[1] Joseph could have easily yielded to her advances. Instead, he set his eyes on the goals he wanted to achieve, the person he wanted to be, and he refused to travel down that side road. When temptation came, Joseph learned how to say "no."

Finally, Joseph was able to say "go." As Joseph continued down the main road of his life, the opportunity God had prepared him for finally opened up before him. At that point, Joseph was able to say "go."

Step three is directly connected with the other two steps. Because Joseph had the patience to say "whoa" when trouble came and because he had the purity to say "no" when temptation came, Joseph had the power to say "go" when the task of his life opened up before him.

Excellence comes in the lives of those who stay on the main road. Mediocrity comes to those who travel the side roads. Because they give up when trouble comes and give in when temptation arises, they give out when the task of their life looms before them.

When Trouble Comes

Joseph's experience is instructive, for we too face trouble. Everyone either is a problem, has a problem, or lives with one! Trouble comes to us all.

Sometimes we have trouble at home. Betty did something that her husband Joe thought was stupid, so he said to her, "Why did God make you so beautiful but so doggone stupid?" Without missing a beat she came back, "I guess God made me beautiful, so you would love me, and he made me stupid so I would love you!"

Trouble also grows out of our parenting role. No task in life is any more challenging and frustrating than being a parent. Danny and David were talking one day. David was obviously distraught. Danny asked, "What's the matter?" David replied, "I'm just upset because my son got his hair cut." "What's wrong with that?" queried Danny. "You've been griping about his long hair, and now he cut it off. That should make you happy. What are you upset about?" David shook his head and answered, "Now I can see his earring!"

Trouble often comes from our work. One employer said to his boss, "If I lose this account, will you still like me?" "Yes," the boss replied. "I will still like you. I'll just miss you."

Trouble! All of us have it. So what do you do when the side road of trouble looms large before you?

First, *remember that you are not alone.* Misfortune strikes in every person's life. Trouble is a universal experience of human-kind.

Take Joseph, for example. Repeatedly, the biblical writer said about him, "The Lord was with Joseph." However, even the presence of God in his life did not screen him from disappointment and pain. Joseph was a man—God's man—who nevertheless knew the experience of misfortune.

Or take the apostle Paul. Second Corinthians 12 highlights the misfortunes that struck him. Someone has suggested that the way Paul knew if he had a good day on Sunday was to count his bandages on Monday. Suffering was his everyday companion. Add to that the mysterious "thorn in the flesh," and you have the testimony of another man—God's man—who was nevertheless slapped in the face by life.[2]

When suffering comes, accept it as a part of life on this earth.

Second, *remember that the immediate evaluation of any situation is not always accurate.* Joseph could have given up at any point along the way. When he was thrown into the pit by his brothers, he could have moaned, "This is terrible." When he was sold as a slave, "This is terrible." When he was betrayed by Potiphar's wife, "This is terrible." When he was tossed into jail, "This is terrible." That would have been his immediate evaluation in each experience. Later on, however, when he was able to put it all in perspective, he told his brothers, "And now do not be distressed, or angry with yourselves, because you sold me here; for God sent me before you to preserve life."[3]

This is what Joseph meant. Had he not been sold into slavery, he would never have met Potiphar. Had he not met Potiphar, he never would have met Potiphar's wife. Had he not met Potiphar's wife, he never would have been put in jail. Had he not been put in jail, he never would have met the Pharaoh's baker. Had he not met the Pharaoh's baker, he never would have been asked to interpret Pharoah's dream. Had he not become his interpreter, he never would have been made prime minister of Egypt. Had he not been the prime minister, he never would have been able to save his family and ensure the continuing line through whom God would eventually complete His redemptive work.

The immediate evaluation and the final evaluation were altogether different. Remember that when trouble comes.

Third, *remember where you are going.* Since trouble plagues every person, trouble obviously does not have to prevent a person from reaching his or her goal. What is important, then, is not what happens to you but what happens to what happens to you. Not outward circumstances but inner commitment is the key.

A father wanted to encourage his son who was upset about his schoolwork. "Just don't give up," the father encouraged. "Remember, Robert Fulton didn't give up. And Thomas Edison didn't give up. And Albert Einstein didn't give up. And then there was Irving McPringle." "Who is Irving McPringle?" came the reply from the boy. To which the father responded, "See, you never heard of him. He gave up!"

Life's productive people are not those couched in comfort and planted in prosperity but those who have been able to endure patiently and persistently push forward in the midst of adversity. They refused to give up.

Orenthal Didn't Give Up

Orenthal grew up in the ghetto of San Francisco. Rickets softened his bones and made them weak. Soon his legs began to bow under the weight of his body. His mother didn't have enough money for doctors or braces, so she rigged up some homemade contraptions. Nothing worked. Orenthal suffered physical deformity from his disease.

To compensate for his physical weakness, Orenthal presented a rough, tough exterior. Street fights were a common occurrence in his youth. Three times he was arrested. The broad road of trouble seemed to be the main road of his life. However, Orenthal recognized it as a side street and he refused to take it. Instead, he stayed on the main road which eventually led him to his goals.

What could a boy from the ghetto with a physical deformity and social disruption possibly accomplish? How about the Heisman

Trophy and a place in the permanent record books of professional football? For this Orenthal is Orenthal James Simpson—better known as O. J.[4]

What was his secret? He had the patience to stay under the load and persist until he transformed tragedy into triumph and problems into possibilities.

A Kicker with Half a Foot

When the phone rang, Joe Ed Hawkins told me he had a friend he wanted me to meet. The friend was Tom Dempsey. He lived in New Orleans and was in the car business. But, in most people's minds, that name Tom Dempsey is not connected with the car business. His name is a legend in the National Football League as a kicker. Do you remember his story?

Tom Dempsey was a kicker with half a foot. He was born with only half a right foot and a twisted right arm and hand. Even a successful career in college did not entice the professional teams to draft him. They insisted he wasn't professional material. His strong belief that he could play professional ball led eventually to an opportunity. The rest is history.

Detroit and New Orleans were fighting it out in a close game. The Saints saw victory going down the drain when the Lions' kicker put the pigskin through the uprights for a field goal with eleven seconds left in the game. The score was 17-16 in Detroit's favor. After the kickoff, in two plays and nine seconds, the Saints took the ball to their own 45-yard line. The coach sent Tom Demsey in to attempt a field goal. The ball was placed on the ground 63 yards away from the goal post! When the ball touched ground again, it had passed through the uprights for a victory and a field goal that continues to stand as the National Football League record.

What was his secret? Dempsey explained, "I have never learned to give up. So many times in life and in sports, I have seen things turn around because someone has perservered, someone has kept faith."[5]

When Temptation Comes

Even after you avoid the side road of trouble, you are not home yet. The side road of temptation will also appear. So how do you handle temptation?

First, *prepare for it before it comes.* The time to deal with temptation is before you have to face it. If you wait until temptation comes to decide what you are going to do about it, that's too late. The prior decision that you are going to stay on the main road is the key to avoiding this side road.

A little boy was sitting on the fence beside the road with his eye on the luscious red apples hanging on a nearby tree. The farmer in the field noticed from a distance, so he drove his tractor over to where the boy was. "Young man," he quizzed, "are you trying to steal an apple?" "No, sir," the boy returned, "I'm trying not to steal an apple."

The way not to steal an apple is not to stare at the apple in the first place. Look at the apple long enough, and the deed will eventually be done. On the other hand, if you keep your eye on the main road, the power of the apple will be decreased. When temptation comes, ask yourself the question, "What do I want for my life?"

Second, *remember that every action has consequences.* When temptation comes, do not simply consider the action you are tempted to take. Take the long look and think about the consequences which will inevitably follow if you take that action.

Remember that while you are free to choose your actions you are not free to choose the consequences of your actions. Every person is a prisoner of his own experience. Many of us spend six days sowing wild oats and then go to church on Sunday and pray for a crop failure! The truth is that consequences inevitably follow actions.

When you face temptation, ask yourself the question, "What will be the results in my life if I take this step?"

Third, *promptly and decisively resist temptation when it comes.* Look at Joseph. Potiphar's wife said, "Let's go to bed." Joseph

said, "I'll see you later."[6] When temptation comes, deal with it instantaneously. Immediately remove yourself from the circumstances producing the temptation. He who hesitates is lost.

When temptation comes, ask yourself the question: "How can I get out of this?"

No sooner will you move past the side road of trouble than the side road of temptation will appear. Learning how to say no to the side roads is the essential step in being able to say yes to the main road.

Flexibility Is the Key

Joseph teaches us another lesson. What enabled him to achieve excellence in the midst of trouble and temptation was his ability to adjust to the ever-changing circumstances of his life. Flexibility was the key.

Life's circumstances are constantly changing for all of us. The comfort and security of childhood are replaced by the competitiveness of the adult world. Financial security is often replaced by financial setbacks. Temporary achievements are often followed by failures. Each change in our lives can propel us onto a side street if we are not able to adjust.

College superstars know the reality of this drastic change in circumstances. Each year a small group of college basketball players have the spotlight of the nation focused on them as they participate for what is known as The Final Four. These are the final four teams playing for the National Basketball Championship. What happens to these athletes who are surrounded by the hoopla of Final Four mania after the spotlight is removed?

USA Today polled 238 players who participated in at least one of the NCAA Final Four Championship games from 1977 to 1986. The survey indicated that an amazing number of these athletes have been able to match their achievement on the basketball court with continued excellence in life.

What is their secret? The pollsters concluded that those who make it in school "seem able to channel the athletic lessons of discipline and self-sacrifice into their academic lives."[7] Then, after college, they are able to shift chunks of their athletic experience to life, realizing the things that made them successful in sports are the same things that will make them successful in life: discipline, team work, and self-sacrifice. In other words, they are able to adjust to their changing circumstances.

What Do You Do When a Door Closes?

The year was 1904. The event was the Louisiana Purchase Exposition in Saint Louis. The local folks called it the Saint Louis World's Fair. Hundreds of vendors were set up at the fair, among them one selling waffles and another selling ice cream. Then, the waffle vendor had a problem. He ran out of plates, and none of the vendors would share their inventory of plates with him. The door was closed. Failure seemed inevitable.

Instead of staring at the closed door, the waffle vendor suddenly spotted an open door that he had not seen before. The ice-cream man offered to sell him some ice cream at a discount, providing the waffle man the opportunity to make a little money to cover his losses. That is when the open door was spotted. The waffle man made a batch of a thousand waffles, pressed them thin with a flat iron. Then, while they were still hot, he rolled them into a circular cone with a point at the bottom. The next day, he sold the ice cream piled up in his twirled waffles, and the ice-cream cone was born![8] Like thousands before and since, this man achieved excellence because he refused to go down the side road of trouble but insisted on staying on the main road.

The sister of William James provided another example of one who stayed on the main road. Her physical handicap could have prevented her from enjoying her life. But it didn't. Why not? William James wrote of his sister that "she never accepted the horizon of her invalidism."[9]

E. Stanley Jones, world missionary, exhibited the same spirit. Trouble often hounded him in his search for excellence. How did he deal with trouble in his life? He pointed out that he got hold of a principle and a power that was to be the driving force of his life. "I wouldn't bear opposition and difficulties," he stated, "I would use them."[10]

Trouble was no side road for E. Stanley Jones. Rather, it was another lane on the main road that led him toward his ultimate goal of magnifying God with his life.

A One-legged Football Player

Carl Joseph was a star football player for the Madison High Cougars in Madison, Florida. One game film showed Joseph, nose guard on the Madison team, fighting off blockers and making one tackle after another. When he was knocked down, he would hop back up. Then he'd go in for the tackle.

On one particular play, the opposing quarterback was back to pass. Forced out of the pocket, he began to scramble. Joseph bullied his way out of the jam of players and followed in hot pursuit. He dove and tackled the fleeing quarterback. Another sack for Joseph.

Carl Joseph was an all-around athlete for the Cougars. He could dunk the basketball. He high-jumped five feet ten inches. He won thirteen varsity letters in high school. In the homecoming game his junior year, he made twelve tackles and led his team to a 6-0 victory.

What's so unusual about all of this? This Carl Joseph had only one leg! With that one leg, this young man decided to avoid the side road of self-pity or self-defeat. Instead, he stayed on the main road toward excellence.[11]

Points to Remember

Deciding what you want in life is only the first step in achieving excellence. Many have started out chasing a stag and have ended up watching a mousehole. So remember:

1. Your circumstances can be obstacles or opportunities: it's up to you.
2. The temptation to be less than your best has to be confronted continuously.

3. Trouble is an inevitable part of life for all of us.
4. The immediate evaluation of our circumstances is not always accurate.
5. Excellence comes to those who persist in the midst of adversity.
6. Prepare for temptation, so when it comes, you can decisively resist.
7. Flexibility is the key.

Excellence comes to those who are able to avoid the side streets.

4
I Thought It Was a Lion, Too

The seven-year-old son came running into the house and interrupted his mother's bridge club by shouting, "There's a great big, huge, enormous lion out in the front yard!" A quick glance by the mother revealed the animal in question was not a lion but the neighbor's cat. Embarrassed by the intrusion and feeling that she had to do something, the mother addressed her son, "Warren, you know we don't tell lies at our house. Go to your room." Then, perhaps because all of the ladies of the bridge club were watching, she added this flourish, "Maybe it would be a good idea if you had a talk with the Lord about that."

The boy left but did not stay gone more than a few seconds. "Well," replied one of the ladies, "that was quick. What did God tell you?"

"Oh," answered the grinning youngster, "He said, 'Don't worry about it, Warren. When I first saw it, I thought it was a lion, too!' "

This story illustrates a vital truth about life: people see things in different ways. I have discovered that the level of a person's accomplishments and the quality of his life will be determined by how he sees things.

After you have decided where you want to go and have avoided the side roads that would lead you astray, how then can you most fully realize your goals? Focused vision is the key.

So here is the third principle for achieving excellence.

LEARN HOW TO SEE THINGS AS THEY CAN BE

A Man with a Vision

Elisha was a remarkable man for many reasons. I think the most remarkable thing about Elisha was his vision. He had twenty-twenty vision spiritually. Elisha could see things that other people could not. That vision was the key to his marvelously productive life.

On one occasion, Elisha was in Dothan.[1] The king of Syria was bothered by Elisha's interference, so he sent his horses and chariots and a massive army to capture Elisha. They came by night and surrounded the city where Elisha was. Elisha's servant saw the army circling the city and cried out, "Elisha, what are we going to do?" Elisha responded, "Don't worry, because those who are with us are more than those who are with them."[2]

The servant took another look. He did not see what Elisha saw. So the mighty prophet of God prayed, " 'O Lord, I pray, open his eyes that he may see.' And the Lord opened the servant's eyes and he saw; and behold, the mountain was full of horses and chariots of fire all around Elisha."[3]

Elisha and his servant illustrate the two different kinds of people in the world. The difference is in how they see things.

The Problem or the Problem Solver

The servant focused on the problem. He saw the armies of the enemy and cried in despair, "What are we going to do?"

Many people are stifled in life because they see only the problems. Husbands and wives do not enjoy marriage because they see only the problems. Employees do not enjoy their jobs because they always talk about the problems. Young people do not develop their gifts because they think only about the problems. Most people, like the servant of Elisha, see only the problems.

Elisha was different. He focused not on the problem but on the problem solver. He looked out the same window and saw the same situation. What was his response? "Don't worry," he said, "we've got more going for us than going against us."

Robert LeTourneau, dynamic American businessman of a few years ago, captured the same idea when he testified, "God is my partner. How can you ever be afraid with a partner like that."[4]
Which do you see in life: the problem or the problem solver?

The Obstacle or the Opportunity

When the servant asked Elisha, "What are we going to do?" he was not seeking information. He was expressing an opinion. He was declaring that the surrounding enemies of Syria presented an insurmountable obstacle that would keep him from reaching his goal.

That is the philosophy of many today. They see obstacles all around. And they explain their failure in life by alibiing, "Life was against me. I didn't have a chance." Or, "My high school principal had it in for me." Or, "I was born with a handicap." Or, "My parent died when I was just a child." Or, "I've had a health problem all my life." Or, "My husband left me." Or, "My wife deserted me, and I was devastated." Or, "My business failed, and I could never get over it." Like the servant of Elisha, they allow their problems to become obstacles which stop them dead in their tracks.

Elisha was different. He saw his problem not as an obstacle but as an opportunity. Consequently, he took the steps to transform adversity into advancement.

The wife of author Nathaniel Hawthorne expressed the same idea. After Hawthorne lost his position in the customs house, he came home utterly defeated. He declared to his wife that he was a failure. "Nonsense," she retorted. "Now you can write your book." And he did. Under her inspiring encouragement, Hawthorne wrote one of the classics of literature: *The Scarlet Letter.* Why? Because he was able to see a problem in his life not as an obstacle but as an opportunity for advancement.

How do you see your problems: as obstacles or as opportunities?

After viewing the scene of the surrounding armies, the servant came to Elisha not to seek his advice but to announce that they would soon be defeated by the invading army of Syria. "It's all over," he cried, "we are defeated."

The world is filled with people who expect defeat in life. A youngster complained to his dad, "I'll never understand these math problems. They are so confusing. I can't make any sense out of them at all. I think I'm going to fail my test tomorrow."

Seeking to encourage him, the father counseled, "Son, you've got to be positive."

"OK," replied the boy, "I'm positive I'm going to fail the test tomorrow."

Many approach life like that. They know they are going to fail. They expect to be defeated. The enemy is so great. The problems are so insurmountable. There is no way they will ever win.

A sign on an office wall professed: "When one resigns to fate, his resignation is accepted." What an accurate description of the servant of Elisha! The enemy surrounded him, so he resigned to fate, and his resignation was accepted.

Elisha was different. Because he focused on the problem solver instead of the problem, because he saw the problem as an opportunity rather than an obstacle, he anticipated victory instead of defeat. "Don't worry," Elisha replied to the servant, "those who are with us are more than those who are with them."

An army sergeant expressed the same idea. In the heat of the battle, he gathered his troops around him. "All right, men," he declared, "we are completely surrounded by the enemy. Let's not let a single one of them escape."

The same choice faces you. You can focus on the problem, be stopped by the obstacle, and end up in defeat. Or, like Elisha, you can focus on the problem solver, be stimulated by the opportunity, and move forward to victory. The difference is how you see things.

From Invalid to Legend

Wilma was born premature which led to complications with pneumonia. Then a bout with polio left her leg crooked and her foot twisted inward. She had to wear leg braces for the first eleven years of her life. Her only traveling away from home was the weekly bus trip to Nashville where she received treatments for her leg. She didn't get a good start in life. Yet, even during those early years in braces, she suggested to her mother that someday she would make a special contribution to life.

At the age of eleven, Wilma began to take her braces off when her parents were gone. Painfully, she would hobble around the house. After a year of this secret therapy, she confessed to the doctor what she was doing. He told her she could take off the braces occasionally. When she went home that day, she took the braces off. And she never put them on again.

She tried basketball, and within two years she became the number-two girl on the team. While playing basketball Wilma caught the attention of Ed Temple, track coach of the Tennessee State Tigerbelles. He invited her to try out for the track team. In her first race, she beat everyone in the race. Soon she beat every girl in the state of Tennessee.

At the age of sixteen, Wilma tried out for the Olympic team and made it. In the 1956 Olympics she was eliminated in the semifinals of the 200-meter dash. She did bring back a medal as a part of the third place 400-meter relay team. She was not satisfied with her performance. She assured herself that next time she would do it right.

To prepare for the 1960 Olympics, Wilma doubled up on her training. In addition to the regular workouts at the school, Wilma would sneak out of the dormitory to run on the track two hours each night. At sunrise, she would be at it again. And again at ten. And again at three. She followed this schedule for four years.

When she walked out on the stadium field in the summer of 1960 in Rome, Wilma was ready. She electrified the crowd with easy victories in the 100- and 200-meter dashes. Then, she anchored the United States team to a first place finish in the 400-meter relay. Three gold medals! And each race was won in record time!

At the age of eleven, Wilma was a little crippled girl, hobbling around on her braces, isolated from the world. Nine years later she "owned the world," for Wilma Rudolph had become a living legend.[5]

What was her secret? She saw herself as a winner, and then she became what she saw herself to be.

Boy, Is This My Lucky Day!

What determines whether a person sees the problems or the problem solver? The opportunity or the obstacle? Victory or defeat? The key is your attitude. Your attitude is the mind's paintbrush, the window through which you view the world around you.

David, a second grader, was bumped while getting on the school bus and suffered a two-inch cut on his cheek. At recess, he collided with another boy, and two teeth were knocked loose. At noon while sliding on ice, he fell and broke his wrist. His father noticed David was clutching something in his hand. "What is it?" the father asked. David replied, "It's a quarter. I found it on the ground when I fell. This is the first quarter I ever found. Boy, is this my lucky day!"

The problems and hurts were there, but this young man had discovered the key to excellence—the ability to focus on the blessings rather than the burdens of life. David was an optimist.

Criticism is often directed at the optimist. The optimist is labeled as naïve, idealistic, and out of touch with reality. Optimism does not, however, ignore the problems in life. Optimism simply refuses to believe that the problems tell the whole story. Optimism sees an opportunity in every calamity. In contrast, pessimism sees a calamity in every opportunity. Which one is more realistic?

Is it more realistic to begin the day by saying, "I know I am going to be a miserable failure today," or by saying, "I believe this is going to be my day"?

Is it more realistic to say as you stand before an immense opportunity "I can't" or to say "I can"?

Is it more realistic to focus on the problem and give up or to stand before a problem and focus on the possible solutions?

Some people see nothing good, like the pessimist who went duck hunting one day with an optimist. The optimist had the smartest, most-expensive hunting dog in the state. He trained the dog to do things no other dog could do. The two men sat quietly behind the duck blind. Suddenly, the ducks arrived. Bang! Bang! Bang! Both men emptied their guns, and several ducks fell into the water. The optimist ordered his dog, "Go get 'em." The dog leaped from behind the blind, ran out on top of the water to the floating ducks, picked them up, ran back on the water, and carefully laid them in a line by his master's feet.

"Well," bragged the optimist. "What do you think of that?" The pessimist scowled, "Some dog! He can't even swim, can he?"

Which is more realistic: the bruised boy with a quarter saying, "This is my lucky day!" or the pessimist witnessing the marvel of a dog walking on water and complaining that the dog can't swim?

It is not a matter of being realistic. It is a matter of developing the proper attitude.

Attitude Adjusters

So, how can we develop the proper attitude? How can we face life with confidence?

1. *Begin with a personal inventory.* Think of your eyes. Over 300,000 separate telephone lines connect your eyes to your brain so you can see.

Think of your ears. The average piano has eighty-eight keys. Yet, in your ear you have 1,500 keys to provide the ability to hear.

Think of your heart. Less than six inches by four inches in size, the heart beats at least seventy times a minute, 100,800 times a day. If you live to be seventy years old, your heart will beat 2,575,440,000 times.

Think of your brain. Within its three pounds are thirteen billion nerve cells, almost three times as many cells in one human brain as there are people on the earth. Billions of protein molecules in the cells of the brain enable you to file every perception, every sound, every taste, every smell, and every action you have ever experienced, witnessed, or even thought about.

Biochemist Harold J. Morowitz of Yale University estimated the chemical value of the human body. He arrived at the average value of $245.54 per gram in the human body. Weighing in at 168 pounds, he calculated his "dry" weight at 32 percent of that since we are 68 percent water. This meant that his dry weight was 24,436 grams. Multiplying this times the $245.54 per gram, Morowitz estimated his chemical value at $6 million. To synthesize these chemicals for basic raw materials would run their value to $6 billion. Morowitz estimates assembling them into cellular structure would run to $600 billion![6] Recognizing our assets is the first step in developing the right attitude.

2. *Think about your achievements.* An inventory of yourself will help you recognize your assets. A victory list will help you properly evaluate your achievements.

Remember the times when you achieved something. You made a good grade on a test. You won an award. You successfully completed a task. You ministered to a need in someone else's life. Everyone can make such a list. Realizing the things you have already accomplished in life will motivate you in a positive way.

3. *Study the lives of those who have overcome obstacles to achieve excellence.*

Remember Helen Keller who refused to let her blindness and deafness prevent her from achieving excellence. She not only overcame her obstacles, she was thankful for them. She wrote on one occasion, "I thank God for my handicaps for through them I have found myself, my work and my God."[7]

Remember Yogi Berra, Hall of Fame baseball star for the New York Yankees. When he showed up at Yankee Stadium in 1947, he was slow and small. His throwing was wild. Once when he fired toward second base to put out a runner stealing second, he hit the pitcher in the chest. Another time he beaned the second base umpire who was standing ten feet from the bag. But Yogi kept

working. He spent extra hours in the batting cage. He studied rival hitters until he knew their every weakness. Consequently, Yogi became one of baseball's greatest players, playing on fourteen pennant-winning teams, winning Most Valuable Player honors three times, setting eighteen World Series records.

Remember Margaret Mitchell. She wrote a novel which was turned down several times. Publishers declared it had no appeal. At long last, the book was published. The title of this oft-rejected novel: *Gone with the Wind.*

Remember a bachelor in a large Southern city. He bequeathed his vast fortune to the three women who turned down his invitation to marriage. He explained in his will, "To their refusals I owe all my worldly happiness!"

These are not fairy tales. They are true-life stories of men and women who were confronted by obstacles but transformed their obstacles into opportunities. If they did it, so can you. Feed your mind with these examples.

4. *Seek the company of happy, positive, enthusiastic people.* Some people I avoid like the plague. They are a pessimistic, negative, nit-picking kind of people. When I spend too much time with them, I become pessimistic, negative, and nit-picking. I constantly seek the company of other people because their positive, enthusiastic, optimistic spirit never fails to inspire those same qualities in me.

Phillips Brooks, an Episcopal preacher from Boston in the nineteenth century, was not only a gifted pulpiteer but also a powerful personality. One man who was inspired by his presence stated that Phillips Brooks demonstrated "the contagion of a triumphant life."[8]

5. *Spend time talking to yourself.* Denis Waitley has written, "Every winner I've ever met in every walk of life, male or female, uses the technique of mental simulation every day to modify his or her own self-image."[9]

Some of you may be saying, "Talk to myself? You've got to be kidding!" The fact is you do talk to yourself every minute of the day. About every action, after every task, following every word—

in the midst of every relationship, you are evaluating yourself. This evaluation has a tremendous impact on your life. Since you are talking to yourself all the time anyway, you should make the self-talk positive, affirming, and encouraging.

In the 1976 Olympics, hurdler Guy Drut was France's only hope for a track-and-field medal. He was greatly influenced by skier Jean-Claude Killy. Drut explained, "Jean-Claude told me I was the only one who knew how to get my body and mind to their ultimate peak for the Olympic Games. He then told me that after I had done this that I should keep saying to myself, 'I have done everything I can do to get ready for this race and if I win, every-thing will be great, but if I don't win my friends will still be my friends, my enemies will still be my enemies, and the world will still be the same!' I repeated this sentence to myself before the qualifying heats and during the break between the semifinals and finals. I kept saying the sentence over and over and it blocked out everything else. I was still repeating it to myself when I went up to get my gold medal."[10]

Through self-talk, Guy Drut kept his attitude clear and posi-tive, and that upbeat attitude contributed to his achievement of excellence.

The Choice Is Yours

Your attitude toward life is determined, in the final analysis, by a choice on your part.

Two men bumped into each other one day in a railway station in Austria. One was an alcoholic, begging for enough money to buy one more bottle of wine. The other man responded by asking how a person had come to the place of existing from one drink to another. The beggar responded that from the beginning, the cards of life had been stacked against him. His mother had died when he was very young; his father had beaten him and his brothers and sisters mercilessly. Then World War I came along and the family was separated. "You see," explained the beggar, "I never had a chance. If you had grown up as I did, you would be this way, too."

The other man replied, "This is very strange. The truth of the matter is that my background is very similar to yours. I, too, lost my mother when I was young. My father was also a brutal man, often beating me and my brothers and sisters. The war also separated me from my family. However, I felt I had no choice but to try to overcome these circumstances rather than being overcome by them."

As the two men continued their conversation they made a remarkable discovery. They were, in fact, blood brothers, long separated by the trauma of war!

Two human beings came out of the identical set of circumstances, yet one ended with a life of excellence and the other with a life of despair. What was the difference? The way they saw life.

Points to Remember

People do see things in different ways. A vital step in achieving excellence is to develop the proper vision. Remember:

1. How you see things will determine what you do and eventually what you become.
2. Every circumstance can be either an obstacle or an opportunity, depending on how you see it.
3. Your vision will be determined by your attitude toward life.
4. Optimism is the most realistic approach to life, for it motivates you to move past your problems to solutions.
5. You can adjust your attitude by taking a personal inventory, making a victory list, learning from other achievers, spending time with positive people, and talking to yourself.
6. Your attitude will not be determined by outward circumstances but by an inner choice.

Excellence comes to those who learn how to see things as they can be.

5
An Important Lesson from Gooch

Jim was not sure why he hired Gooch as a salesman for his company. He did not seem to have the qualifications. If murdering the English language were a crime, Gooch would be on death row. But Gooch had a uniqueness about him that motivated Jim to give him a chance. What a wise decision that turned out to be!

At the end of Gooch's first week on the field, he sent Jim this note: "Dere Bos, I seen this outfit which they ain't never bot a dimes wuth of nuthin from us, and I sole thim a cuple of hundred thousand dolars wuth of guds. Now I'm gwine to Chawgo." The letter was signed, "Gooch."

Two days later, a second letter arrived at the home office from the field. It read: "Dere Bos, i cum hear and sole them half a milyon." The letter was signed, "Gooch."

The next day, the boss posted both letters on the bulletin board with a note which went: "We ben spendin' to much time hear trying to spel insted of trying to sel. Let's watch these leters from Gooch who is on the rode doing a grate job for us. Go out and do like he dun." It was signed: "Bos."

Sometimes, the reason we do not achieve excellence is that we spend too much time trying to spell instead of trying to sell. We become so caught up in the paralysis of analysis that we never get around to doing anything. Step number four in achieving excellence can be simply stated:

A Child Shall Lead Them

Most people are familiar with the biblical character named Moses. He led the parade of Hebrew heroes in the Old Testament. His brother Aaron, though lesser known, is still familiar to most of us. But what do you know about Miriam? This sister of Moses and Aaron spent her life under the shadow of her two famous brothers who dominated the attention and drew the affection of the Hebrew people during the most crucial period of their history. Yet, living under that kind of pressure, Miriam nevertheless became one of the most renowned Hebrew women of all time.

Her eventual greatness is foreshadowed in a vignette from her childhood. The Hebrews lived in Egypt at the time. Because of the rapid increase in the number of Hebrews, the Egyptian Pharaoh wanted newborn Hebrew boys to be killed. The account of how Moses was hidden in a basket for his safety, adopted by the daughter of the Pharaoh, and thus spared for God's mission is one of the most familiar and exciting of all biblical stories.[1]

Miriam played a key role in this deliverance. She watched the basket in which her brother had been placed for safety. When Moses was discovered by Pharaoh's daughter, Miriam suggested that she needed a Hebrew woman to care for the baby. When Pharaoh's daughter agreed, Miriam summoned her mother who was then commissioned to take care of her own baby by the daughter of the man who had ordered all Hebrew boys to be killed!

What does this have to do with us today? Miriam demonstrated an important principle for achieving excellence. What did Miriam do? She acted. She did something. She was given a seemingly small opportunity, and she made something big out of it.

How Big Do You Have to Be?

How big do you have to be before you can accomplish something with your life? The fact that prevents many from achieving excellence in life is their feeling of insignificance. *Who am I,* they ask themselves, *to think I can accomplish something with my life?*

A young man took a personality test to determine how he could deal with his "inferiority complex." The counselor reported the results of the test: "The tests indicate that you do not have an inferiority complex. You are simply inferior!"

Many feel that way about themselves. They believe they are too insignificant to achieve anything. How big do you have to be before God can use you?

A church in Florida sponsored a Week of Champions in their church one year. They invited Christian athletes from all over the country to share their testimonies with the youth of the city. Each night large crowds gathered in the school auditorium for these special services. One of the guests was Paul Anderson, touted at that time to be the strongest man in the world. The thrust of his testimony was, "If the strongest man in the world needs Jesus, so do you."

A couple of weeks later a young man told the pastor of the sponsoring church he had decided to become a Christian. The pastor asked him when he made the decision. The young man explained that the decision was made on the night Paul Anderson gave his testimony. The pastor wanted to know what Paul Anderson said to convince him of his need for Christ. The young man answered, "I don't remember what Paul Anderson said. What touched me was a paraplegic being pushed forward in his wheelchair during the invitation time to accept Jesus. I said to myself that if God could do something for him, then surely he could do something for me."

The strongest man in the world was in the auditorium that night, but God used a paraplegic in his weakness to lead the young man to Christ.

How Big of an Opportunity Do You Need?

Many are stymied in their quest for excellence not by their lack of personal power but by the size of the opportunities around them. Their rationalization goes about like this: "I know I could accomplish something with my life if I just had a big enough opportunity. If I had a big job to do, if I had an outstanding

opportunity for service, then I could really achieve excellence."
How big of an opportunity do you need to accomplish something
significant in your life?

In the British West Indies, the construction of a church in one
of the villages came about in an interesting way. For years, missionaries visited the village. Each year, many were converted to
the Christian faith. In those periods of religious enthusiasm, the
people talked about building a church. However, before they gathered the stones, their fervor would cool, and the church would not
be built.

One ten-year-old boy in the congregation, Peter, heard the plea
to build a church. He watched the men pick out a lot on which
to construct the church. He heard the new Christians make plans
and then watched as the enthusiasm waned, and the plans were
left unfulfilled. But Peter decided he would not let the work stop.
He had to pass the vacant lot selected for the church site every day
on his way to school. He decided that he would carry a large stone
each day and throw it onto the lot. The other boys in the school,
noticing what Peter did and thinking it would be fun to throw a
stone onto the empty lot, began helping him with his work. Finally, a huge pile of stones stood in the center of the lot.

When the men of the village saw the gradually rising pile of
stones, they were ashamed. "If the children of our village can do
this much to build a church," they figured, "surely we can do the
rest." So they bought cement and wood and glass, and, eventually,
a beautiful church stood in the center of the village. Why? Because
a ten-year-old boy was willing to act.

What Keeps Us from Acting?

What keeps us from acting when the opportunities of life are all
around us? One of two factors is usually involved.

Fear often keeps us from taking advantage of our opportunities.
Grandma was finally persuaded by her family to fly from her
home down South for a visit. She dreaded the experience, so when
she arrived at the airport, her family was anxious to hear her
comment. "How was your flight, Grandma?" they asked. "It was

OK, I guess," she replied, "but I never did put my full weight down!" People go through life like that. They miss the joys of life's opportunities because fear paralyzes them and keeps them from putting their full weight down.

A second hindrance to action is *procrastination.* Mark Twain once suggested, "Never put off until tomorrow what you can put off until the day after tomorrow." Such is the approach of procrastination. The word comes from two Latin words, *pro* meaning forward and *cras* meaning the morrow.

"I'll do it tomorrow" is the motto of many people. They even procrastinate about joining the Procrastinators' Club of America. According to a newspaper article, the club claims a nationwide membership of over 500,000, although only about 33,500 have actually sent in the membership application. A member thought to be sending Christmas cards early one year was expelled from the club. He was later reinstated, however, when they found out the cards were for the previous year. One man vowed to quit smoking. He knew it would be easy for him because he had never taken time to start smoking![2]

The world provides many gorgeous locations in which to live, but the most unproductive place in the world is "Someday I'll." Whenever confronted by a challenge or an opportunity, some people avoid it with the promise, "Someday I'll . . ." The residents of "Someday I'll" never experience the exhilarating achievement of excellence.

Two Kinds of Fear

Fear is a barrier on the road to excellence. What do we fear?

Sometimes, *fear of failure* prevents us from taking the action that would lead us toward excellence. In our day of success orientation, failure has become one of life's most dreaded labels. There is a difference between failing and being a failure.

Babe Ruth struck out more times than anyone who has ever played the game of baseball. A strikeout is definitely a failure at the plate. However, no one would consider Babe Ruth a failure.

Ty Cobb was thrown out trying to steal more than any other

baseball player in history. To attempt to steal a base and then to be thrown out is definitely a failure. However, no one would consider Ty Cobb a failure.

The salesmen who achieve the most sales usually have the most rejections. Every rejection is a failure. But, when you evaluate the life of these leading salesmen you would not consider them failures.

Someone has analyzed failure as fitting into five categories. A person may fail because he has chosen the wrong work. Failure might come through the lack of discipline. A person may fail because he wishes to fail. In some cases, failure comes through a tragedy beyond the person's control. The fifth category is a failure that comes when a person is trying new and untested ways of expression.[3]

When you fail trying to match the practice of your life with your potential, when you fail trying to stretch yourself toward new achievement, when you fail trying to experience excellence—that is not failure!

To realize that the ultimate failure in life is simply to do nothing, say nothing, and be nothing can liberate us from our fear of failure and can mobilize us into action.

Ironically, at times the barrier to action is the other side of the coin. Often, *fear of success* is the barrier that prevents us from moving toward excellence.

Denis Waitley has written, "After years of study and some painful experience of my own, I am convinced that people often procrastinate and resist change because they are afraid of the perceived 'costs' of success." Then, Waitley lists these "costs": the bad habits we have to give up, the pressure of being an example for others, the willingness to separate from a peer group which holds you back, the untested territory you have to explore, the hard work that is demanded, and the criticism and jealousy which often ensues.[4] To be willing to move from mediocrity to excellence, from the way things are to the way things can be, does cost. But the reward is incomparable.

To realize that the cost of excellence does not compare to the reward of excellence can liberate us from our fear of success and can mobilize us toward action.

Rudyard Kipling once said that we have reached manhood when we can "meet with triumph and disaster and treat those two imposters just the same."[5]

Coping with Fear

Fear can at times be a positive motivator. Fear is behind every notable achievement of mankind. Fear of ignorance led to the public school system. Fear of disease led to medical research. Fear of darkness led to the development of the electric light. Fear of exposure led to the construction of houses. Fear is at times an instructor of great sagacity. Fear at its best summons forth new energies, produces life's most valuable achievements, and protects from life's severest hazards.

However, when it is allowed to escalate into what psychologists call the fear spiral, fear becomes a negative force which immobilizes us in the face of life's responsibilities and prevents us from achieving excellence.

How can you cope with fear?

First, *analyze your fear.* What is the source of your fear? Is your fear based on objective fact? Is the fear justified? Analyze the fear. Analyzing your fear will enable you to distinguish between the fear emotion and the fear object. In many cases, you will discover that the fear is imaginary.

Take a look at your fears. Is there anything to them? Or are they simply figments of your imagination?

Waitley cites a University of Michigan study which determined that 60 percent of our fears are totally unwarranted. Twenty percent have already become past activities and are thus out of our control. Another 10 percent are so petty they don't make any difference anyway. Of the remaining 10 percent, only 4 to 5 percent are real and justifiable.[6]

Some of our fears are justified. These we must concentrate on. But realize the truth of this statement: many times the thing we need to fear the most is fear itself.

Second, *focus on others.* Confront fear with love. What does love have to do with fear? Why is compassion an antidote for anxiety? Because fear often grows out of an unhealthy focus on self: self-love, self-concern, self-centeredness, self-protection. Fear is rooted in the concerns: "What will happen to me? What will others think of me?" Love changes the focus. Love causes us to look at others, and it asks the question, "What can I do for them?" That's why a mother deathly afraid of fire will nevertheless rush into a flaming house to rescue the child she loves. Love makes us forget self for the sake of others. "There is no fear in love but perfect love casts out fear."[7]

Do It Now!

Procrastination also prevents us from reaching excellence. Why do we procrastinate? Because we do not understand the value of time.

A traveler noticed an unusual scene as he traveled down a country road, so unusual in fact that he stopped to investigate. He saw a farmer on a ladder holding a pig in his arms. The pig was eating an apple hanging on a tree. The traveler watched for a moment and finally commented, "What are you doing?" The farmer responded, "I'm feeding my pig." "Won't that take a long time?" queried the stranger. "Maybe so," replied the farmer, "but what is time to a pig?"

To a pig, time may not mean anything. But to a human being, time is the essence of life. Thoreau once stated that we cannot kill time without injuring eternity.[8] I would expand his statement to conclude that you cannot kill time without preventing excellence. No one lives long enough to waste the days you have. No one is rich enough to buy back your past. No one is strong enough to reclaim a lost opportunity.

Carl Riblet, Jr., said, "There are four kinds of thief—the love thief, the embezzler, the base runner safe at second, and the thief who steals your time. The latter is the worst thief because, while love can be replaced, stolen gains can be repaid and the base runner put out at third, time can never be renewed."[9]

Because time waits for no one, the time to move into action is now.

Making a List

How can you cope with procrastination?

First, *plan your daily activity.* Some lay out their plan for the day on the prior evening before going to bed. Others spend the first part of the morning planning their day. Whatever time works best for you, make a list of things to do, people to call, and tasks to accomplish every day.

Then, *prioritize those plans.* Mark those activities which will be most productive. Give high priority to those responsibilities which will cause problems if left undone. Assign a high priority to those tasks that will best enable you to reach your goals.

After making the list and prioritizing the plans, begin with the highest priority items. Work through the list, one item at a time. Check off each item as completed. Make a list and then live by the list.

Sound simple? Yes, it does. Yet, incredibly, so few people take these simple steps which will motivate them to action.

In a dream, an angel told a man that a sum of $1,440 would be deposited in the bank for him each morning. He could use the money for anything he wanted, on one condition. At the close of each business day, any balance not used would be canceled. It could not be carried over to the next day, but a new $1,440 would be credited to him.

He awoke to face a new day and realized what the dream meant. Every day life credited his account with 1,440 minutes. Each night those minutes not invested in some good purpose would be canceled.

Excellence comes to those who wisely invest the 1,440 minutes each day.

The Tragedy of Inaction

Inaction prevents excellence because it cuts with both sides of the blade. Inaction deprives us. It deprives us of the opportunity to expand, the chance to achieve, and the thrill that comes from victory. It therefore prevents us from achieving excellence.

The tragedy of inaction goes deeper. It not only keeps us from achieving excellence but also robs others of the impact our loving service can have on them.

Someone captured this truth in poignant prose:

"I was hungry and you formed a humanities club and discussed my hunger. Thank you.

"I was imprisoned and you crept off quietly to your chapel and prayed for my release.

"I was naked, and in your mind you debated the morality of my appearance.

"I was sick and you knelt and thanked God for your health.

"I was homeless and you preached to me of the spiritual nature of the shelter of God's love.

"I was lonely and you left me alone to pray for me.

"You seem so holy, so close to God. But I'm still very hungry, and lonely, and cold."[10]

The most important achievement in life is not success. The most important achievement in life is to move out of the passive voice into the active voice.

Still Tying Shoes

The animals in the jungle decided to have a football game. The problem was that no one could tackle the rhinoceros. Once he got a head of steam, he was unstoppable. Consequently, when he received the opening kickoff, he rambled for a touchdown. The score was 7 to 0. No one scored the remainder of the first quarter. In the second quarter, the other team tied the score 7 to 7. Despite the lion's warning, the zebra kicked the ball straight to the rhinoceros again. Sure enough, the rhino caught the ball and was racing for another touchdown. Suddenly, he was brought down with a vicious tackle. When the animals unpiled, the lion discovered that a centipede had made the tackle. "That was fantastic," congratulated the lion. "But where were you on the opening kickoff?" The centipede replied, "I was still putting on my shoes."

The game of life is passing rapidly by while many of us are still trying to put on our shoes. Excellence comes to those who are willing to get into the game.

Points to Remember

A well-known leader was once asked, "What does it feel like to wake up one day and realize that you are famous?" He responded, "One thing is certain. If a person becomes famous, he has not been asleep."

Excellence does not come to those who sleep. It comes to those who are willing to act. So remember:

1. Achieving excellence is not determined by how big a person is. Excellence is, therefore, an attainable goal for every person.
2. Excellence is not made possible by the opportunities outside a person but by the determination inside a person.
3. What we must fear is not the failure of achievement but the failure to attempt achievement.
4. The cost of excellence is far outweighed by the reward of excellence.
5. Whether or not we achieve excellence will be determined by what we do with our time.
6. The journey of life begins with the step we are willing to take right now.

Excellence comes to those who are willing to act.

6
The Best of Things
in the Worst of Times

The townspeople were in total despair. A fire which started in a diner was threatening to burn down the entire shopping district. They seemed helpless to do anything about it. Suddenly, a truck filled with farm workers came speeding down a hill toward the fire. The crowd moved back as the truck drove into the flames. The workers jumped out and beat at the fire with their coats, miraculously bringing it under control. The city fathers were so grateful for the men's heroism that they gave to each a plaque and a $1,000 reward.

After the ceremony, a newsman interviewed the driver and asked him what he was going to do with the money. Without a moment's hesitation the man replied, "You can be sure the first thing I'm gonna do is to fix the brakes on my truck."

Is that what leads to excellence in life? Faulty brakes which force us unwillingly into the heat of the battle? No, it goes deeper than that. Excellence is not achieved accidentally. Excellence does not come simply because we set goals for our lives. Nor will properly envisioning these goals automatically bring excellence. After establishing the goals, we must move forward. After envisioning these goals, we need to move into action.

The question is, "How can we move forward at the proper time and in the proper way? How can we be ready to move into action?" The answer is found in our habits. We will do in an emergency what we have already been doing prior to the emergency.

So here is the fifth principle in achieving excellence in today's world:

DEVELOP GOOD HABITS

In the Worst of Times

In a cemetery in England, a tombstone has this epitaph etched upon it: "In the worst of times, he did the best of things." What an accurate description of a man by the name of Daniel. Daniel "had it made" during his earlier days. As a fifteen-year-old boy, he was selected from among the royal sons of Judah for a special program of education and enlightenment in the courts of Babylon. Although he was forcefully seized from his homeland, this was nevertheless an honor, for King Nebuchadnezzar had specifically ordered that only boys who were physically fit and mentally bright should be chosen. Daniel's selection, therefore, underscored the potential of his life.

Success marked his earlier days in Nebuchadnezzar's court. He was an administrator, an interpreter of dreams, a man of deep intellect. Those were the good days.

Then a crisis developed. The Babylonians were replaced by the Persians as the world power. Nebuchadnezzar and Belshazzar were replaced by Darius. Love for Daniel was replaced with jealousy.

Daniel's enemies were determined to discredit him. Unable to find any fault in his public service, they sought to destroy him on the basis of his private devotion. They persuaded Darius to issue an edict whereby for thirty days everyone was to worship the king only. Any break from this rule, and the offender would be fed to the lions.

These were the worst of times for Daniel, a time of crisis, for this edict of the king stood in direct opposition to Daniel's allegiance to his God. What would he do? The biblical writer tells us: "Now when Daniel knew that the document was signed, he entered his house . . . and he continued kneeling on his knees three times a day, praying and giving thanks before his God, as he had been doing previously."[1]

The end of the story can be succinctly summarized. Daniel was arrested, thrown to the lions, but spared by the power of God. In the end, what appeared to be Daniel's final hour became, in fact, his finest hour. In the worst of times, Daniel did the best of things.

What was his secret? A key phrase in the above description of Daniel sums up the whole story. When the crisis came, Daniel prayed and gave thanks "as he had been doing previously." Daniel had instituted some customs in his life, some holy habits to which he daily gave himself. These habits enabled him to do his best even when the worst came.

The Difference Between Success and Failure

Og Mandino is one of the most popular authors in our day. His book *The Greatest Salesman in the World* tells the intriguing story of a man named Hafid to whom were given some special scrolls. These scrolls contained the principles which, if inculcated in his life, would enable him to become the greatest salesman in the world. He was given nine scrolls with nine principles. The tenth scroll contained the secret of learning.

The first principle written upon the first scroll was this: "I will form good habits and become their slaves." In discussing the power of habit in shaping our lives, Mandino reached this conclusion: "In truth, the only difference between those who have failed and those who have succeeded lies in the difference of their habits."[2]

What a truth! Whether or not you are your best has nothing to do with your abilities. Whether or not you are your best has nothing to do with your intelligence. Whether or not you are your best has nothing to do with your circumstances. Whether or not you are your best depends on your habits.

Incorporate into your life holy habits that shape you and mold you into the image of God, and you will be your best, even in the worst of times. Fail to incorporate into your life the customs that will conform you into the image of God, and you will muddle along in mediocrity, regardless of the circumstances.

What are the customs to which you give yourself on a regular basis? What habits dominate your daily schedule? The answer to those questions will determine your achievement in life for, like Daniel, those who are their best are those who are shaped by holy habits.

Do You Have a Price?

Where do you start in developing the proper habits? The place to start is with a conviction that controls your life. What is a conviction? A conviction is not something you hold—it is something that holds you. A conviction is something that makes you a convict. You can't get away from it. You cannot be disloyal to it. A conviction is a principle that permanently resides in your heart and perpetually shapes your life.

Is there a conviction in your life that sustains you in times of crisis? Is there a principle to which you are so deeply committed, a belief to which you are so closely tied, that nothing or nobody can cause you to move away from it?

A minister and a young actress happened to be sitting by each other at a large dinner party. As they talked, the conversation focused on the changing morals of our time. The minister said to the young actress, "Let me ask you a question. Would you live with a man if he offered you a million dollars?"

The actress responded affirmatively. "Of course I would. A girl would be a fool not to."

The minister continued, "Would you live with the same man if he offered you $5.00?"

"Of course not," she responded indignantly, "what kind of woman do you think I am?"

The minister replied, "We have already established what kind of woman you are. The only thing we are trying to determine now is your price."

Do you have a price, or is there a conviction to which you are so deeply committed that it is beyond any price?

Men and Women with a Conviction

The men and women of history who have made the most significant contributions to life have been possessed by a great conviction.

Jonathan Edwards inaugurated the great spiritual awakening in colonial America because he was possessed by a conviction. "Resolved that all men should live to the glory of God," he wrote in his diary at the age of nineteen. Then he added, "Resolved, second, that whether others do this or not, I will."[3] Jonathan Edwards was possessed by a great conviction.

William Booth's marvelous work with the Salvation Army was motivated by a conviction. He wrote in the autograph album of King Edward VII these words, "Some men's ambition is art, some men's ambition is fame, some men's ambition is gold, my ambition is the souls of men."[4]

The same truth appears in the lives of men and women in every field.

One of today's most prolific writers is W. Phillip Keller. His books on faith as seen through the eyes of nature have been phenomenally successful, particularly *A Shepherd Looks at Psalm 23*. In his autobiography, Keller describes the beginning of his writing career. His desire to write motivated him to use his spare time to produce a book manuscript. He worked on it for hundreds of hours. He explained, "I would actually write and rewrite steadily for the next eleven years of my life before a single line was ever accepted for publication." Why did he do it? Because of a conviction that drove him.[5]

Few have earned universal acclaim like Paderewski whose name became synonymous with excellence on the piano. He would often play a bar of music forty or fifty times before a performance to get it right. After playing before Queen Victoria, he received this word of praise: "Mr. Paderewski, you are a genius." Paderewski responded, "That may be, but before I was a genius I was a drudge." Why such discipline? Because of the conviction which controlled him.[6]

Thomas Edison's name is synonymous with excellence. He was a workaholic before that term was vogue. His wife constantly besieged him with her desire to go on a vacation. Finally, Edison gave in. To his wife he said, "OK, I'll go. Where do you want to go?" She responded, "Decide where you would rather be than anywhere else on earth, and go there." "Very well," he replied. "I'll go there tomorrow." He woke up the next morning, and went back to his workshop![7] Why? Because of the conviction that possessed him.

The truth applies in every field. Excellence begins with a conviction.

Paying the Price

Conviction alone will not lead to excellence. Conviction must be manifest in discipline.

Babe Didrikson Zaharias was one of the greatest female athletes of all time. A man, attending a golf clinic led by the Babe, asked her how he could learn to hit the golf balls like she did. She answered, "Simple. First you hit a thousand golf balls. You hit them until your hands bleed, and you can't hit any more. The next day you start all over again, and the next day and the next. And, maybe a year later, you might be ready to go 18 holes. And after that you play every day until the time finally arrives when you know what you are doing when you hit the ball."[8]

Excellence costs. A price has to be paid. Don't think that a conviction is sufficient to lead to excellence. A conviction is the starting point. You must then build from that conviction a framework of discipline. You have to pay a price.

A colorful old Cajun always wore a necklace made of alligator teeth. A visitor who spotted the Cajun asked him about his necklace. "These are alligator teeth," the Cajun explained. The stranger responded, "Oh, I understand. That's like a string of pearls people wear in other parts of the country." The Cajun countered, "Only difference is anybody can open an oyster."

Anybody can be mediocre. Excellence comes to those who are willing to meet the alligators of life face-to-face.

A Basketball Android

"Pistol" Pete Maravich was inducted into the Basketball Hall of Fame in 1987. He rewrote the NCAA scoring records as a collegiate averaging 44.2 points per game in his four years at Louisiana State University. During his ten year professional career, Maravich averaged 24.2 points and 5.4 assists per game.

When asked the reason for his excellence, Maravich called himself a "basketball android" as a boy. He explained, "I even took a basketball to bed with me until I was 14 years old. I would just lie there in bed throwing it up and doing fingertip drills. When I was 8 and 9 years old I would dribble the ball 2 ½ miles into town and 2 ½ miles back. When I got a little older I would dribble it into town while riding my bike. Whatever I did, wherever I went, I had the basketball with me. It just became an extension of my hand."[9] Any wonder he was a magician with the basketball?

Excellence is not automatically achieved. Excellence is a by-product of discipline. Discipline provides the impetus to repeat an activity until it becomes ingrained in our lives as a habit.

Then Comes the Payoff

Those who achieve excellence do not focus on the price to be paid but on the payoff to be enjoyed.

The baseball player hits a home run because of extra batting practice. That's the payoff. The receiver catches the touchdown pass because he spent an hour every day after practice catching balls. That's the payoff.

Convictions provide discipline. Discipline produces habits. Habits then liberate us to achieve excellence.

Excellence is the payoff. It comes as a result of habits. You form good habits, and then your habits form you.

From Fame to Shame

Habits shape our lives whether they are good or bad habits. The result of good habits is excellence. The result of bad habits is self-destruction.

Stephen Foster was blessed with a superb gift of music. Witness his songs, "Oh! Susanna," "Jeannie with the Light Brown Hair," "My Old Kentucky Home," and hundreds more, sung by every generation since the middle of the last century. No doubt Stephen Foster was gifted. He had such potential. But he died in 1864 at the age of thirty-eight. He died without a friend, as a charity case in the Bellevue Hospital in New York City, stone drunk with a slashed throat, with only thirty-eight cents in his pockets.[10]

What happened? Why this wasted life? He did not channel his potential into the grooves of habit which would perpetuate his contributions through a lifetime. The lack of discipline and the absence of healthy habits led to Stephen Foster's downfall.

Take a Survey

Look at your life. What do you see? What are the habits that shape your life? If you look closely, you will probably discover three kinds of habits: good habits, bad habits, and good habits which no longer serve any useful purpose.

Billy watched his wife as she cooked a ham. This was the first time Betty had ever fixed ham. Before putting the ham in the pan, Betty cut off both ends. "Why did you do that?" he asked. "I don't know," she responded. "That's the way Mother did it." Betty's mother happened to be visiting, so Billy went into the den and asked her why she cut off both ends of the ham before she put it in the pan. "I don't know," she replied. "That's the way my mother did it." Billy was really intrigued by now. So he picked up the phone and called Betty's grandmother. "Why did you cut off both ends of the ham before you cooked it?" Finally, the mystery was solved. The grandmother explained, "The pan I had was so small that I had to cut off both ends of the ham to fit it into the pan." Two generations of women had followed this habitual way of cooking ham although the conditions had changed.

Each of you has things that you do certain ways, habits you follow, even though the reason for doing them that way has long since been removed. Make a list of the habits of your life. Write out beside each one the reason you follow that particular habit and the result it brings in your life. Since our habits shape our lives we need to make certain that they are the right habits which bring the right results and are done for the right reason.

Just Trust the Lord

The Methodists were gathered for a gigantic camp meeting which featured some of the finest preachers in the state. One of the ministers called in sick. He explained he would not be there to deliver his assigned message. The bishop called a young minister aside and asked, "I want you to preach the message right after lunch today." The young preacher was a basket case. "What am I going to preach, Bishop? I don't have a sermon with me. I'm not prepared. What am I going to preach?"

The bishop replied in a very dignified and pious voice, "Just trust the Lord, young man. Just trust the Lord."

The young preacher was desperate. He did not know what to do. As he stood there in the camp office pondering what to do he spotted the bishop's Bible on one of the shelves. He thumbed through it for a text. Instead of just a text, he saw some typewritten notes which were obviously a sermon. The sermon sounded great, so taking the bishop's Bible and the notes, he went to the service. The young preacher amazed everyone with his sermon. They were thrilled. After the service they flocked around this young preacher to commend him for his sermon. He impressed everyone except the bishop. The bishop pushed his way through the crowd, "Young man," the bishop thundered. "You preached my sermon that I was going to preach in the closing session tonight. Now what am I going to do?" The young man replied with dignity, "Just trust the Lord, Bishop. Just trust the Lord."

Trusting the Lord does not mean you do nothing and expect God to provide everything for you. Trusting the Lord does not mean you can approach life unprepared and still expect to experience excellence. Trusting the Lord means that you do everything you can, develop a vision of what you want to be, institute the habits that will shape you in a positive way, and then you apply discipline. Then just trust God to make good on His promise.

Points to Remember

Joe arrived home to witness a shocking scene. His wife's car was almost totally demolished. The back fender was smashed in. One side was dented. The other side had scratch marks. The front fender was pulled loose on the left side. The car was a wreck. He ran into the house and exclaimed, "Betty, what in the world happened to the car?" She answered, "I backed out of the garage this morning and hit the side door, scraped against a tree, hit the mailbox, and then smashed into the fire hydrant on the other side of the street." "Then what happened?" the concerned husband queried. She responded, "Then, I lost control of the car!"

Control comes through the discipline of habits. So remember:

1. The foundation of discipline is a conviction which captures you.
2. Conviction is not enough unless it is channeled into specific disciplines in your life.
3. The reason so few achieve excellence is that they are unwilling to pay the price that discipline demands.
4. Habits begin with a single action but are then built through repetition.
5. Discipline is possible for anyone at any time.
6. Habits do not constrict your life, but rather they liberate you to experience real life.

Excellence comes to those who establish healthy habits.

7
Nothing Could Stop Him

George Cafego was a splendid halfback during the early days of professional football. He played for the old Brooklyn Dodgers football team. One day, in a game against the New York Giants, Cafego brought the ball upfield practically by himself. Just before the half ended, he broke away over left tackle. First one man hit him, then another, but Cafego kept going. Another man hit him and twisted him around, but Cafego kept going. Finally, about five Giants ganged up on him. Still he plowed goalward. At last he started down, just as the timer's gun exploded. "My soul!" shouted a spectator. "They had to shoot him to stop him!"

Those who slide through life without making an impact on life are those who turn from the dock just as their ship is about to come in. They lack the key ingredient of persistence. The single most important factor in achieving excellence is the ability to let go of yesterday and move toward tomorrow by concentrating on today. So here is principle number six in achieving excellence:

> REFUSE TO GIVE UP

Transformation Followed By Continuation

No greater man has been included in the ranks of Christianity than the man named Paul. His transformation on the road to Damascus is so well known that it has provided an expression used and understood even by those outside of Christian circles. A "Damascus-road experience" is a term used to refer to any dramatic change in a person's life. Paul was aggressively seeking to destroy the Christian faith. When he had his encounter with Jesus Christ on the Damascus road, his life was dramatically changed. That transformation was the foundation of his productive life.

To understand fully the dynamic of Paul's life you have to go beyond the Damascus-road experience described in the Book of Acts and hear his philosphy of life declared in his letter to the Christians at Philippi. Here it is: "Brethren, I do not regard myself as having laid hold of it yet; but one thing I do; forgetting what lies behind and reaching forward to what lies ahead, I press on toward the goal."[1]

Transformation was the foundation of Paul's life. But the explanation for his life of excellence is that his transformation was followed by continuation. Three steps were involved.

First, *he knew how to forget.* Paul canceled out of his mind anything in his past which broke his pace or lessened his speed in the present.

He forgot his accomplishments of the past. Paul had a life full of mountaintop experiences to which he could have retreated. He could have spent the final years of his life watching reruns of his past victories, but Paul knew how to forget his accomplishments of the past.

He forgot his hurts of the past. His life was filled with trial and turmoil. Open hostility followed him each step of the journey. He often was hurt, physically and personally. Paul could have nursed those hurts and sulked in his hatred and expended his energy in plots for revenge. But he didn't. Why? Because he knew how to forget.

He also forgot his failures of the past. Think of Paul's past. Remember the harm he had done to the cause of Christianity. He had participated in the death of Stephen, the first Christian martyr.[2] He had arrested many Christians and persecuted others. He could have protested, "God can't use me. I have blown my opportunity." But he didn't, because he knew how to forget.

Paul's past was marked by spiritual victories and spiritual defeats, by personal friendships and personal feuds, by healing relationships and hurtful ones. But that was his past. It was gone. It had already been entered into the logbook of life. So Paul forgot it.

Second, *he knew how to concentrate.* Paul's priority punctuated this proclamation of his philosophy of life: "This one thing I do," he declared. One translation puts it like this: "I am bringing all my energies to bear on this one thing."[3] Call him a fanatic if you want to, but the point is that Paul knew how to concentrate.

A fanatic is a person who will not change his mind and will not change the subject. That was Paul. There was one subject about which he talked, one desire by which he was motivated, one purpose for which he lived, and that was to magnify this One who had changed his life. He brought all of his energies to bear on that one thing. He knew how to concentrate.

Third, *he always reached out for tomorrow.* Paul proclaimed this philosophy of life to the Philippians near the end of his days. Remember what preceded this proclamation. Remember all the flourishing churches he had organized, all the Epistles he had written, all the significant accomplishments he had made. As we see him sitting in the prison at Rome near the end of his life we want to insist, "Paul, you've done enough. You can ease off now. Just take it easy. Just coast on in."

What did Paul say? Paul said, "I do not regard myself as having laid hold of it yet," so "I press on toward the goal."[4] Paul was aware that there were always more mountains to climb, more lives to help, more churches to build, more personal victories to win, more sermons to preach, more work to be done. He was aware that there was much of the race still to be run, so he kept running.

Cancellation, concentration, and continuation—those were the pillars of Paul's philosophy of life. Driven by those forces, Paul refused to give up.

Making a List

The dog came out of nowhere and bit the lady as she was taking her afternoon walk. The pain was severe, but she did not go to the hospital. Several days later, the bite was even more painful. Finally, she decided to go to the doctor. After examining her the doctor told her, "I have some bad news for you. The dog that bit you evidently had rabies, and you are not going to make it." A few minutes later, the doctor came to check on her and found her writing something down. "Are you making a will?" the doctor quizzed. "No," she responded, "I'm making a list of the people I want to bite!" Just a joke, but it makes a point.

How much personal energy is expended making lists of the people we want to get even with? But every moment spent plotting revenge is a moment wasted. Every ounce of energy spent sulking over the past is energy that cannot be used surging toward the future. Time wasted getting even cannot be used to get excellence.

All of us have hurts. In the process of living and relating, hurt often results. That is something over which we have no control. We can control, however, how we will react to that hurt. We can spend our time making lists and plotting our revenge, or we can learn how to forget.

Troubled Twins

Billy and Willie, twin sons of a merchant out in the Midwest, grew up as inseparable companions. They did everything together. Thus, no one was surprised when both chose not to get married. Instead, they went to work in their father's store and, when he died, they took it over. They operated the business as partners.

One morning a customer came into the store and bought a dollar's worth of merchandise. Billy waited on the customer, laid the bill on top of the cash register, and walked to the door with the customer. A few moments later he remembered what he had done, but when he went to the cash register, the dollar was gone.

He asked Willie if he had put the dollar in the cash register. Willie declared he had not seen the dollar. Billy mused, *"That's really funny. I distinctly remember putting it on the cash register, and no one else has been in here but you and me."*

Perhaps if the matter had been dropped then, nothing would have come of it. Unfortunately, Billy brought it up again about an hour later. "Willie," he said, "are you sure you didn't do something with that dollar bill?" This time a barb of accusation was included in the comment. Willie picked up on the tone and reacted sharply. A fight ensued, and for the first time in their lives, a serious breach opened up between the brothers.

On several occasions they tried to deal with the matter. Every time the realities of suspicion and outrage took deeper root. Finally, the hurt was so deep and the suspicion so strong that they dissolved their partnership. A partition was drawn down the middle of the store. Billy and Willie became vicious competitors with each other. Neither would speak to the other. Each tried to turn the people of the community against the other. What had been a model of harmonious relationships became a running sore which infected the entire community.

Then, after twenty years of polarization and bitterness, an incredible thing happened. A well-dressed stranger from out of the state drove up and entered one of the stores. He asked Billy how long he had been in business at that location. When he found out it was over twenty years, he reached into his pocket and confessed, "Then you are the one with whom I must settle an old debt." He then proceeded to relate how twenty years before he had been a drifter passing through the town. He continued, "I had not eaten for two days. I had no money. I remember walking down the alley back of the store and looking in the door. I saw a dollar bill on the cash register. I had never stolen anything before in my whole life, but that morning I was so hungry I yielded to temptation. While the clerks were up front, I slipped in and took the dollar. That act has weighed on my conscience ever since, and I decided I would never have any peace until I came back and made amends."

With that, the stranger tried to hand Billy a large bill, but he couldn't, for Billy was literally dissolving in tears. All he could say was, "Come next door with me. I want you to repeat that story to someone else."

When he told Willie the story, both men began to weep uncontrollably, not so much about what the stranger had done to them, but what they had done to each other in response to his action.

Twenty years of estrangement, hatred, suspicion, and poisoned relationships—all because of two brothers who were not able to forget.

Holding onto the past hurts, successes, and failures will put excess baggage on your shoulders. Excellence comes to those who, like Paul, know how to forget.

Running for His Life

Picture the scene. Alabama and Auburn were playing in one of the most crucial games of the year. Alabama was leading by five points. Two minutes were left in the game. Alabama had the ball twenty yards away from the goal line. On first down, the number-one quarterback was injured. Coach Bryant sent in his number-two man. Before sending him in, Bryant gave him strict instructions. He was not under any circumstances to throw the ball. He was to run the ball three downs, even if they did not gain a yard. By that time, the game would be almost over, and the defense would hold them. On second down, Alabama was stopped dead. On third down, they gained a yard. Fourth down. The quarterback turned to hand off the ball but missed the hand off. He began to run, and when he did, he spotted a receiver open in the end zone. What a chance to lock the game up. He could not resist the chance to be a hero, so he lofted a pass to his open receiver. What he did not notice was the safety for the other team only a few yards away. This all-American safety happened to be the fastest man on the field. As soon as the ball was in the air, the safety cut in front of the receiver, pulled the ball in, and headed for the other end zone. All of a sudden, like a flash of lightning, the quarterback caught up with the swift safety and tackled him on the two-yard line just as the clock ran out. Alabama won. After the game, the Auburn coach asked Bear Bryant, "I've read the scouting reports. That quarterback is supposed to be slow. How is it that he caught up with the fastest man on the field?" Bear Bryant replied, "It's simple. Your man was running for a touchdown. My man was running for his life!"

Motivated by the desire to stay alive, that slow quarterback focused all of his energies on one object. He was able to concentrate.

Releasing the past is not enough. Releasing the past enables you then to focus on the present. As you focus on the present, the key is concentration. What keeps most of us from achieving excellence is not lack of desire but lack of concentration. Our time, energy, money, and interests are diverted in a hundred different directions.

In every area of competition, concentration is the key. In the final moments of a basketball game, the team that usually wins is the one able to keep its concentration. The receiver who catches the winning touchdown pass is the one who is able to concentrate on the ball and watch it into his hands. The baseball player who gets the game-winning hit is the one who is able to concentrate.

The same truth applies to our lives. Concentration is the key. When you learn how to focus your attention on your immediate task and refuse to be sidetracked by other opportunities, problems, and challenges, then you are on the road to excellence.

From Hobo to Hero

Art Linkletter's name is a household word in America. Did you know that he started out as a hobo, traveling from place to place as a stowaway on the train? From that inauspicious beginning, Art Linkletter has achieved a life of fame and fortune. Entrepreneur, entertainer, author, world traveler, spokesmen for many great causes—Art Linkletter's life is marked by excellence in every endeavor he has undertaken.

What is his secret? Certainly not his background. His circumstances were less than ideal. He is obviously a gifted man but no more gifted than many. How was he able to achieve so much in his life?

Linkletter answers the question in his autobiography. He wrote, "The word *persistence* is the key to my whole survival ethic. If I have made my mark in the entertainment field, in business, and, in a more private way, in sports, it is because I persisted often when others of equal or superior ability fell by the wayside. A canceled sponsor, a dry oil well, an inglorious slide down a ski slope on my rear and—each setback spurred me on to try again and do better."[5]

Releasing the past and concentrating on the present establishes the platform for the final step: continuation. Many people have learned how to forget. Many have discovered the secret of concentration. The final ingredient that enables some to achieve excellence and not others is the ability to persist until the job is done or the goal is reached.

Listen to the repeated testimony to this truth.

Alexander Graham Bell is a name we immediately connect with the telephone. The telephone, however, was only one of his inventions. His creative mind produced invention after invention for over sixty years. How did he do it? He once testified, "The ideas which I use are mostly the ideas of other people who don't develop them themselves."[6]

Paul Harvey is one of the most respected men in America. His unique style and creative mind have enabled him to reach the top as a commentator. What is his secret? Harvey testifies, "Someday I hope to enjoy enough of what the world calls success that somebody will ask me, 'What's the secret of it?' I shall say simply this: 'I get up when I fall down.' "[7]

Benjamin Disraeli was the only man to be born a Jew who became prime minister of Great Britain. For nearly fifty years, he was a political force in Britain. How was he able to exert such vast influence? Disraeli declared, "The secret of success is constancy to purpose."[8]

The late Ray Kroc, as chief executive officer of McDonald's, was known as America's hamburger king. On his office wall hung this philosophy of life: "Press on: Nothing in the world can take the place of persistence. Talent will not; nothing is more common than unsuccessful men with talent. Genius will not; unrewarded genius is almost a proverb. Education will not; the world is full of educated derelicts. Persistence and determination alone are omnipotent."[9]

Over and over again from those who have achieved excellence

comes this testimony: a big shot is just a little shot who kept shooting!

The Sub Who Became the MVP

Rich Neuheisel realized a dream when he enrolled at UCLA. He did not have a football scholarship, but he became a member of the team as a walk-on. The first two years he played on the scout team. Because of his faithfulness to the team, he was given a scholarship after the second year. Rich began his fourth year at UCLA as the number-three quarterback. Two outstanding quarterbacks were ahead of him, and, consequently, he played very little that year. Because he had redshirted one year (to give him an extra year of eligibility), Rich came back for a fifth season with the Bruins. He was listed as the number two quarterback. At the beginning of the season, the number-one quarterback was knocked out for the year. After five years, Rich finally had his chance. He'd always insisted he could produce if he had a chance. Now his chance had arrived.

The season started slow. UCLA had an 0-3-1 record after four games: no wins, three losses, and one tie. This did not appear to be a championship team.

Rich kept working, kept developing, kept exerting himself, kept learning. At last, UCLA began to win. In the final game of the regular season, UCLA faced the University of Washington for the championship game. UCLA won. In the game, Rich Neuheisel completed 25 out of 27 passes for 287 yards.

This team which played five games before they ever won a single game now was headed for the Rose Bowl. Their opponent was the University of Illinois, ranked number four in the nation after the regular season. What did UCLA do against this team from Illinois? They only beat them 45-9. What did Rich Neuheisel do? He only won the Most Valuable Player award in the Rose Bowl.

Rich Neuheisel could have focused on his past and declared himself a mediocre player at best. He could have focused on his failures. He could have focused on his inadequacies. He could have focused on his hurts he experienced during those four years.

Instead, Rich focused on the future, on what he wanted to become, on what he believed he could become, and he moved on toward that goal. Persistence transformed a walk-own into a MVP.

Points to Remember

Every life is set in the context of these three time periods: past, present, and future. How you relate to these time periods will determine your level of achievement. So remember:

1. The past, whether filled with hurt or marked with success, is unnecessary baggage as we move into the future. Let go of it.
2. Life's greatest challenge is not the choice between the good and the bad, but the choice between the good and the best.
3. A concentration of energy on a limited number of priorities will make your life more productive.
4. The ability to finish a race is more important than a quick start.
5. Nothing in life will take the place of persistence.

Excellence comes in the life of a person who refuses to give up.

8
Anybody Can Answer That

Albert Einstein was one of the most brilliant men who ever lived. His name has become synonymous with genius. Einstein also had a sense of humor. Like the time he was on a tour of universities explaining his theory of relativity. Since Einstein did not drive, he had to be chauffeured from place to place.

One day, on the way to another speaking engagement, the chauffeur said to Einstein, "You know, I've heard this lecture so many times now that I could give it myself." Einstein responded, "Let's see. The people at the next university have never seen me before, so they don't know what I look like. Let me put on your uniform and cap, and you put on my clothes and introduce me as your chauffeur. Tell them that you are Dr. Einstein, and then you can deliver the speech."

The plan unfolded perfectly. No one recognized Einstein incognito in the chauffeur's clothes. The chauffeur was introduced as Dr. Einstein and flawlessly delivered the lecture on the theory of relativity. Then came the unexpected. The two conspirators had not thought about the possibility of questions from the audience. When the chauffeur finished delivering Einstein's speech, a mathematics professor asked a complicated, technical question involving mathematical formulas and language the chauffeur did not understand.

He was equal to the situation, however. After the question, the chauffeur responded, "Sir, the solution to that problem is so simple I am really surprised you would ask me to answer it. Anybody can answer it. In fact," he suggested, "I'm going to ask my chauffeur to come up here and answer it!"

Sometimes you can cover for your lack of knowledge by calling on someone else to rescue you. Most of the time, you have to answer the questions of life yourself. The reason so many people are living beneath their privileges is that they do not have the right answers. They do not have the right answers because they have quit developing their minds. So here is the seventh principle in achieving excellence:

KEEP LEARNING

Apollos Knew Enough to Know What He Didn't Know

I have never known a church which bears his name. Yet, what happened to him needs to happen to most churches today. I have never met a person named for him. Yet, what he experienced needs to be experienced by every Christian in today's church. His name is Apollos. He is the patron saint for those who are good but who want to be better.

Apollos had plenty going for him. He was well educated. As a Jew from Alexandria, Apollos had been educated in the widely respected schools of that city. He had a "golden tongue," able to control an audience with the turn of a phrase. His knowledge of Scripture was expansive. Plus, he was endowed with a spirit of enthusiasm which caused his life to sparkle.[1]

Apollos also had some limitations. Two phrases in the biblical description of Apollos cast a shadow over what otherwise is a bright portrait of a brilliant young Christian. "Being acquainted only with the baptism of John," the biblical writer explained about Apollos, "When Priscilla and Aquila heard him, they took him aside and explained to him the way of God more accurately."[2]

Without going into a detailed discussion of those two phrases, let me simply summarize the situation. Yes, Apollos had a lot going for him, but he also had some limitations. He knew a great deal, but there were some things he did not know.

Picture the scene. Here is Apollos, educated and erudite, hotshot young preacher, holding people spellbound with his eloquence, riding a wave of popularity. Here is this older couple, Priscilla and Aquila, taking him aside and saying, "Apollos, you are so gifted. And God can really use you. But we've noticed some inadequacies, and we'd like to help you."

How would Apollos react? "Inadequacies in me?" he could have protested. "You've got to be kidding." "Me, learn from you?" he could have argued. "Who do you think you are to tell me what to do?" Or he could have argued, "I received my degree from the Jerusalem Seminary. And I was the head of my class. Do you think you have the qualifications to instruct someone of my stature?"

How easy it would have been for Apollos to have responded like that! Instead, Apollos listened and learned, and as a result lived a better life. Why? Because he knew enough to know what he did not know. He realized that all of us have much more to learn about life, so he was willing to keep learning.

God Does Not Need Our Ignorance

John Wesley, founder of Methodism, blended faith and reason into a beautiful balance which provoked some criticism from those suspicious of reason. Carped one critic of Wesley's, "God doesn't need your learning." Wesley retorted, "God doesn't need your ignorance either."[3]

Yet there is an abundance of ignorance floating around. A lady was standing beside the road with the hood of her car raised, obviously stranded. A passerby stopped to see if he could help. "What's wrong?" he asked. She responded, "I don't know. The car just stopped, and I can't get it started." After looking under the hood, the man sat down behind the wheel and tried to start it. He got out and reported to the lady, "Your car is out of gas." She replied, "Will it hurt to drive it home like that?"

Ignorance. Like the young fellow who applied for a job painting the stripe down the middle of a new highway, back before machines were used for that job. The boss offered to give him a trial for the job. The first day, he reported to his boss, "I've painted five miles today." The boss commended, "That's outstanding. Way above average. Keep this up, and you'll have the job." The second day, the worker said, "I painted only three miles today." The boss thought, *Anyone can have a bad day. I'll give him another chance.* When the worker came in the third day he reported, "I painted only one mile today." The boss said, "You're getting worse every day. I just don't think this is going to work out. I'm sorry." As the distraught worker left the office, he shouted over his shoulder to the boss, "It's not my fault that my production level decreases each day. Each day I'm further from the paint can!"

God does not need our ignorance. Instead, he needs men and women who are continually willing to expand their minds with His truth.

The Empty Head

Billy told his mother that he really had a stomachache. His mother explained, "Your stomach hurts because it is empty. It's almost time for dinner, and you haven't eaten in several hours. When you get something in your stomach, it will feel better." About an hour later, the minister stopped by for a visit. "How are you doing today?" the housewife asked the pastor. "Not too well," he answered. "I have a terrible headache." The little ears immediately picked up on that, so Billy said, "Don't worry pastor. Mom says it's because your head is empty. When you get something in it, you'll feel better!"

No part of the human body is more intriguing and marked with more potential than the human brain. Yet, experts tell us that most people in their lifetime use only about 10 to 20 percent of their brain power.

Five percent of the people of the world think. Ten percent think they think. Eighty-five percent would rather die than think!

The mind is a marvelous instrument. We need to put something into it. So how do we do that? What is the key to filling one's mind?

Paul outlined a mental hygiene program in a statement he made to the Christians at Philippi.⁴ Concentration of our minds on six factors will enable our minds to expand.

You need to concentrate on *the truth as opposed to falsehood.* How gullible we are today. We buy things from people we don't know, at prices we cannot afford, in response to advertising we do not believe, to keep up with people we don't even like. To develop your mind, you need to cut through the deceptive, manipulative garble of our day and focus on the truth.

You need to concentrate on *the serious as opposed to the frivolous.* The Greek word for "serious" is the word *semna* which presents the idea of reverence. Have you ever known someone you wanted to ask, "Why don't you grow up? There is more to life than fun and games." That's what Paul is talking about. Growth of the mind comes when you focus your mind on the noble, important, serious matters of life.

You need to concentrate on *the right as opposed to the convenient.* Henry Clay, well-liked statesman of another generation, was a perpetual candidate for president. When he took an unpopular stand on an issue, one of his friends said, "Henry, if you take this position you will never be elected president of the United States." Clay replied, "I would rather be right than be president."⁵

You need to concentrate on *the clean as opposed to the dirty.* The Greek word for "clean" is *hagna* which describes an object so clean that it is fit to be brought into the presence of God for His service. In an X-rated society, perhaps none of Paul's suggestions are more difficult than this. I read about a baker in Dallas, Texas, who makes X-rated cakes. He has sixty-three different designs of dirty cakes!⁶ Mind development comes when we concentrate on that which is pure in an impure world.

You need to concentrate on *the loving as opposed to the discordant.* The word Paul used refers to a kind of attitude which calls forth love from others as opposed to that which causes strife. One guy was called "Whiplash" because he was such a pain in the neck. He was always stirring things up, always creating discord. We need to keep discordant thoughts flushed out of our minds by concentrating on things that create brotherhood.

You need to concentrate on *the positive as opposed to the negative*. The Greek word here means to put the most favorable construction possible on everything, to emphasize what is right about something rather than what is wrong. A mysterious woman of Milan, Italy, traveled the country back in 1977 spreading bad news. She told the people an earthquake was coming. She announced impending doom in one form or another all over the countryside and caused quite a turmoil.[7] Like her, some people key in on the bad news of life. They are negative people because they think negative thoughts. Paul declared that one's mind grows as he concentrates on the positive.

The mind is a terrible thing to waste. Your commitment to excellence in your mind shapes up as you concentrate on the true, the important, the right, the pure, the loving, and the positive.

I Don't Want Johnny to Learn No More

Johnny had just returned from his first day at the city school after growing up in the backwoods. His mother was very skeptical about the school, a skepticism fed by what Johnny told her. He explained all the things he had learned about the human body, and how it is made. The mother called the school and told the principal, "I don't want Johnny to learn no more about his insides."

Formal education scares many people. What part does it play in developing the mind so we can experience excellence? Let me mention two qualifications.

Formal education is obviously not necessary for a person to achieve excellence. History is filled with the names of those who succeeded despite the absence of a formal education. For instance, Eleanor Roosevelt never attended college. Grover Cleveland, Joseph Conrad, and Amelia Earhart never received a college education. Ernest Hemingway missed college as did H. L. Mencken, Rudyard Kipling, John D. Rockefeller, George Bernard Shaw, and Harry S. Truman. High school dropouts who achieved excellence include Henry Ford, George Gershwin, Jack London, Will Rogers, Steve McQueen, and Wilbur and Orville Wright. This list of notables is evidence that a formal education is not necessary to achieve excellence.[8]

Neither is formal education enough in and of itself. Education without morality will not necessarily lead to excellence. We not only need knowledge; but we also need to know how to use that knowledge. Formal education in itself is not enough to enable a person to achieve excellence.

With those two qualifications in mind, the positive conclusion is that formal education can expand the mind and create a desire for excellence.

A young man wrote a dissertation on the influence his teachers had on his life. He wrote of a third-grade teacher whose beauty, charm, and kindness influenced him during his early years. That was the first level, a teacher who inspired love for the teacher. The second level was reached in college when an irascible English professor created within him a love for English literature.

The third level came in graduate school when the young man was working on his dissertation. His major professor was well known and busy and had little time to devote to him. The major professor returned his dissertation with only a few marks on it, but the student was not satisfied. He presented his dissertation to another professor for his comments. Later, he made an appointment with this professor. The professor handed him his manuscript which had pencil marks on practically every page. The professor counseled, "I have read your work carefully. You must rewrite it. Your rhetoric and your expressions are inadequate. Your conclusions and substances are good. But if you want to get the benefit of an education, you will have to rewrite it."

It took the student three months to rewrite the dissertation. The student concluded: "I love that man who lifted me above the love of the person of my teacher and who lifted me above the love of the subject. He, with all his disappointment to me and severe judgment, chastened me to a love of excellence."[9]

When formal education moves a person past love of teacher and subject to love of excellence, then it has made its mark on the life of the student.

Watch the Input

A mother was preparing a green salad for dinner. She had thrown the unusable portions of the vegetables into the sink to be sent down the garbage disposal. Her teenage daughter interrupted her preparation, telling her she and some friends were going to see an X-rated movie. Trying to gain her mother's consent, she insisted that all the kids were going to the movie and that it wouldn't hurt anyone. As the daughter was pleading her case, the mother began to pick up the discarded vegetables from the sink and put them in the salad. Seeing this, the daughter exclaimed, "Mother, what are you doing? You are putting garbage in the salad. That's disgusting." The mother replied, "I figured that if you didn't mind putting garbage into your mind, you wouldn't mind eating it in your salad."

What are you putting into your mind? That is a pivotal question, for what you put into your mind will shape your life.

An ancient proverb suggests, "Sow a thought, reap an action; sow an action, reap a habit; sow a habit, reap a character; sow a character, reap a destiny."[10]

A proverb from the Bible suggests, "For as a man thinks within himself, so he is."[11]

The point of the two proverbs is the same: what you think about and what you allow to enter your mind will determine what you become. Like a giant computer, your mind is recording all of this input, and it will shape your perspective and attitude toward life.

No better illustration of this truth can be found than the spectacle known in history as Watergate. Leon Jaworski, the special prosecutor of the Watergate case, gave this evaluation shortly after the experience: "Still fresh on my mind is the sadness of seeing one of the great tragedies of modern history—men who once had fame in their hands sinking to infamy—all because eventually their goals were of the wrong dreams and aspirations."[12]

Their thinking was wrong, and their wrong thinking led to

wrong actions. What you think will eventually determine what you are.

What Life Has Taught Me Thus Far

Perhaps the most important factor to remember about this learning process is: *is should never end!* You never learn all that you can learn. You never develop your brain as much as it can be developed. No matter how old, no matter how smart, there is always room for improvement.

E. Stanley Jones, the missionary statesman, at the age of eighty-three wrote an autobiography. One of the chapters of his book was entitled "What Life Has Taught Me So Far," because he realized there is always room for improvement.

At the age of ninety-two, Oliver Wendell Holmes, one of the greatest Supreme Court justices of the past, was reading in his library. A friend asked, "What are you doing?" Justice Holmes smiled and answered, "Improving my mind," because he understood there is always room for improvement.

Cato, the Roman scholar, started studying Greek when he was over eighty. Someone asked him why he tackled such a difficult task at that age. He replied, "It's the earliest age I have left," because he realized there is always room for improvement.

The Mind of Christ

There is another factor involved. Because intellectual development without the moral capacity to use that intellect is insufficient, our intellectual development must be brought in tune with the inner spiritual life. An incredible declaration explains the privilege of Christians. The Bible says, "But we have the mind of Christ."[13] When we become Christians, God plants the mind of Christ within us. Every Christian has the mind of Christ. The key to developing one's mind is to bring it in tune with the mind of Christ.

How is that to be done? Again, the Bible presents the guidelines. The Bible says, "We are destroying speculations and every lofty thing raised up against the knowledge of God, and we are taking every thought captive to the obedience of Christ."[14] To bring every thought captive to the mind of Christ is the key step that will liberate our minds to expand.

Points to Remember

The mother was awakened in the night by the cry of her little girl. Rushing into the girl's bedroom, she found her on the floor. She scooped the child up and asked, "What happened?" The girl responded, "I guess I fell asleep too close to where I got in."

That happens to many today. We need to wake up and remember these principles:

1. To achieve excellence demands a growing, expanding mind.
2. To have a growing, expanding mind you must control the input.
3. Formal education can facilitate this learning process, but it is neither necessary nor enough to ensure the completion of the process.
4. Intellectual development without an accompanying moral development will lead not to excellence but to disaster.
5. The end result of true education is a student who loves excellence.
6. What goes into your mind will determine what you are.
7. You never reach a point where you can quit learning.

Excellence comes to those who are willing to keep learning all their lives.

9
That's Quite an Inheritance

The man was on his way to the county fair. He had a chicken in one hand, a pig under his other arm, and a basket on his head. On the way, he became lost. As he tried to decide which direction to take, a lady passed by. "Excuse me, ma'am," he said, "can you tell me how to get to the county fair?" She said, "I sure can. In fact, I'm going there myself, so we can just walk together." She explained, "We are going up this way a mile, then left for a mile, and then left for about half a mile, and we'll be there." "Wait a minute," interrupted the stranger. "Did you say we were going up this way a mile, then left for a mile, and then left for about half a mile?" "That's right," she replied. The stranger made a suggestion. "Wouldn't it be quicker if we just cut through the woods?" The lady protested, "I can't walk through the woods with you. You might try to hug me." The man was stunned. "How in the world could I hug you? I have a chicken in one hand, a pig under the other arm, and a basket on my head?" Without missing a beat, the lady returned, "You could put the chicken on the ground and put the basket over it, and I could hold that little bitty ole pig!"

There is truth in that old story. Everybody needs a hug. In a lonely world, those who reach out and touch someone are creating in life the spirit of excellence. So here is the eighth principle in achieving excellence:

> BE A GIVER

Mr. Encourager

Joseph was the name of one of the greatest heroes of the Hebrews. Joseph was also the name of the earthly guardian of Jesus. Another Joseph in the New Testament came on the scene, although he was not known by his given name Joseph but by a nickname he was given along the way. The early Christians called him *bar Nabas*, "the son of consolation." He was known as "Mr. Encourager."

This was not a nickname capriciously coined but one that grew out of his life. Every picture we have of this man Joseph (called Barnabas) verifies the accuracy of this nickname.

In the earliest days of the church, many needs existed. Some of the first Christians were Jews who traveled to Jerusalem for the Pentecost celebration. When they became Christians, they could not return home, so they stayed in Jerusalem. They had no money, they had no means of income, they were going hungry. Needs existed on every hand. So Barnabas sold a piece of land and gave the money to the church to help meet those needs. It was his practical, tangible method of lending a helping hand. That's our first picture of Mr. Encourager.[1]

Barnabas appears again in relationship to the man named Paul. Paul was the most notorious convert in the short history of the church. This man who had persecuted the Christians now insisted he was a Christian. This man who had opposed the message of Christ now declared he wanted to spread the message of Christ. Everyone in the church was suspicious of him, fearing he had feigned his faith to infiltrate the church, so he could persecute them further. Wait, everyone was suspicious of him, *except* Barnabas the encourager. Barnabas talked in depth to Paul. Then he went to the leaders of the church and confirmed Paul's conversion, persuading them to accept him as a brother in Christ. This encouragement by Barnabas opened the door for Paul's rise to fame as the greatest missionary of the church. It happened because of Mr. Encourager.[2]

Barnabas appears again in relationship to the church at Antioch. Initially, all Christians were converted Jews. Then, the Christian message was proclaimed to Gentiles, and many of them were converted. The Jewish Christians were sensitive about the ramifications of this new development. An evaluation of the situation needed to be made. Who was sent to investigate and encourage these new Christians? You guessed it: Barnabas, the encourager. When he came to Antioch and saw the faith of these new Christians, "He rejoiced and began to encourage them with resolute heart to remain true to the Lord."[3]

Barnabas appears in another crisis situation. He and Paul had just completed their first mission trip, a dramatic success. They had reported to the Christians in Jerusalem, and the sticky issue of relationship between Jewish Christians and Gentile Christians had been settled. Now, Paul and Barnabas were ready to hit the mission trail again. Young John Mark had deserted the mission party on the first trip.[4] As Paul and Barnabas planned for their second trip, Paul refused to allow Mark to go with them. Barnabas, on the other hand, still had faith in Mark. He wouldn't write Mark off. So much was Barnabas determined to encourage Mark that he left Paul and took Mark on a separate mission trip.[5]

Every picture of Barnabas reveals why he was called "Mr. Encourager." He saw the best in others rather than the worst. He encouraged rather than criticizing. He built up rather than tearing down. Barnabas achieved excellence in life not because of what he achieved for himself but because of what he gave to others. He was a giver rather than a taker.

He Saved My Career

In retrospect, we can appreciate the tremendous career of Jackie Robinson who made history in 1947 as the first black baseball player to play in the major leagues. His achievement was not easy, however. From the beginning, people abused him from the stands. Players abused him on the field. He confronted the barbs of prejudicial treatment in every city where the team traveled. Consequently, Jackie Robinson had many rough days.

On one occasion, life seemed to be coming apart at the seams.

The pressure was mounting as the prejudice was continued. Problems invaded his play on the field. In a particular game, Jackie Robinson made two glaring errors. The boos from the stands reached a high decibel level. Pee Wee Reese, the incomparable Dodger shortstop, walked over to Robinson, put his arm around him, and gave him a word of encouragement. Robinson later reflected, "That may have saved my career. Pee Wee made me feel like I belonged."[6]

A sense of isolation plagues many in our day. A little boy returned home after the first day at his new school, obviously dejected. His mother asked, "What's the matter, son?" He answered, "I'm the only one I know at school." Many people feel like that.

Paul Tournier calls loneliness "the most devastating malady of the age."[7] Dr. James Lynch, medical researcher at Johns Hopkins, has written a book on loneliness entitled *The Broken Heart* in which he asserts that loneliness is the number-one physical killer in the world today.[8]

Although one spokesman points out that loneliness is the number-one problem for women in American suburbia[9] and another study designates college students as the loneliest people in the world,[10] the aged seem to be most severely affected by it.

"Miss Victoria" was what everyone called her. She was a long-term resident in a nursing home. Her family never visited her. A volunteer visitor from the local church visited her one day. This was the beginning of a daily sharing time which seemed to bring renewed life to Miss Victoria and always seemed to inspire the gentleman who visited her. After several weeks, Miss Victoria leaned over close to her newfound friend and whispered, "I have a favor to ask." The friend responded, "Whatever you want, just tell me, and I'll do it." She said, "Before I die I want to kiss someone, and I want you to be that someone."

In a world of loneliness, a kiss or a hug or a touch or simply a word of encouragement creates a spirit of love which moves the world toward excellence.

That's Quite an Inheritance

Loneliness is not the only need calling for encouragement. Criticism also creates a need for encouragement. We are living in a negative, critical world. Someone is always ready to point their finger at us and tell us what's wrong with us.

One husband remarked to his wife of six weeks, "Honey, would you mind if I pointed out a few faults I've noticed in you?" "Not at all," she replied, "it was those faults that prevented me from getting a better husband."

Some can come back at criticism like that. For most of us, criticism eats away at our spirit and leaves us discouraged and depressed. How important a word of encouragement is in situations like that.

The minister and his wife slipped away to the mountains for a few days of rest. They wanted to get away from the pressures and relax. They sat down at the restaurant for dinner when they noticed a gentleman going from table to table, greeting the diners. The minister said to his wife, "I hope he doesn't come over here." But he did. He shook the minister's hand and welcomed him to the restaurant. "What is your work?" he asked. "I am a minister," the vacationer answered. The gentleman volunteered, "I've got a preacher story for you." With that he pulled up a chair and began his tale.

"I was born just a few miles from here, across the mountain. My mother was not married at the time, and the criticism leveled at her was also leveled at me. They had a name for me when I started to school, and they used it quite often. I can remember many times going off to myself at recess and at lunchtime because the taunts of my peers cut so deep.

"What was even worse was going to town with my mother on Saturday afternoon. I could feel all of those eyes piercing through me. And I could hear them whispering, 'I wonder whose child he is? I wonder who his father is?'

"When I was about twelve, a new preacher came to the church in our little community. People began to talk about his power and his eloquence and his compassion. I began to go to church myself. The pastor really intrigued me. But I always slipped in late and tried to get out early because I didn't want anyone to see me and say, 'What is a boy like you doing in a place like this?'

"One Sunday, I slipped up. The benediction was over before I realized it, and I found myself in a crowd with the people trying to get out of the building. As I was waiting there, scared to death, I felt a hand on my shoulder. I turned around and there was the preacher, looking through me with those burning eyes. He said, 'Who are you, son? Whose boy are you?' And I thought to myself, *Oh, no, here we go again.*

"But then a smile of recognition broke across his face and he said, 'Wait a minute. I know who you are. The family resemblance is unmistakable. You are a child of God!'

"With that he patted me across the rump and said, 'Boy, that's quite an inheritance. Go and claim it.'

"That one statement," the old gentleman concluded, "literally changed my whole life."

The enthralled minister asked, "Who are you?" The old man replied, "My name is Ben Hooper."

Who was Ben Hooper? This Ben Hooper, born in illegitimacy, went on to become the twice-elected governor of the state of Tennessee. It all began with a preacher in a little country church who dared to be involved in the ministry of encouragement.

There are Ben Hoopers all around us, everyday. Criticism has taken away their spirit and joy. A word of encouragement can put them back on their feet.

Not Right for the Part

Charles Schulz has provided a cartoon strip which enables us to see inside ourselves, for day after day he paints pictures of us in the characters of Charlie Brown, Lucy, Linus, and company. One day Charlie Brown was discouraged, which was not an unusual occurrence. But this time he was really down. When asked what was wrong, Charlie Brown replied, "I'm not worth anything, and it started the day I was born. The moment I was born and stepped on the stage of history, they looked at me and shook their heads, saying, 'Not right for the part.' "

How many people repeat those words to themselves every morning as they look in the mirror is impossible to calculate. Their problem is not social isolation. Neither is it criticism from their peers. Their problem is a low image of themselves.

Some people, of course, are on the other end of the spectrum. For instance, nobody ever accused Teddy Roosevelt of a low self-image. During his presidency, a story circulated about Teddy's first day in heaven. When he arrived, he cornered Saint Peter and snorted, "Your heavenly choir is inexcusably weak! You should reorganize it at once." Saint Peter answered, "All right, you take care of it." Roosevelt ordered, "I need ten thousand sopranos, ten thousand altos, and ten thousand tenors! Can you get them for me?" Saint Peter assured him that he could. "But what about the basses?" Saint Peter asked. Quipped Teddy, "Oh, I'll sing bass!"

A few have that kind of self-confidence, yet most are haunted with the feeling that they are not right for the part. What can break through that shell of self-hatred? A word of encouragement can.

He Made Me Feel Like I Was Somebody

Vince Lombardi engraved his name indelibly into the book of legends in professional football during his career at Green Bay. What was most remarkable about this man was not his victories but the influence he had on the young men who played for him.

One of these was Willie Davis from Alabama. Although Willie wasn't a well-known college player, Lombardi took a chance on him, and Willie came through.

Later, when Vince Lombardi was dying of cancer in a hospital in Washington, DC, Willie Davis flew from California to see him. After only a five-minute visit, Willie flew back to the West Coast. Five days later, he served as one of the pallbearers at Lombardi's funeral at Saint Patrick's Cathedral in New York City. When the reporters heard that this was Willie Davis's second trip across the country in a week, they asked him why he'd come the first time. Everyone knew that Lombardi couldn't last long. Why didn't he just wait until Lombardi died and come for the funeral. Willie's reply was classic: "Listen, man, I had to come. You see, Mr. Lombardi was the first man who ever made me feel like I was somebody."[11]

His Greatest Poem

The celebrated poet Edwin Markham was once asked what he considered to be his greatest poem. Without a moment's hesitation, Markham concluded that the most-treasured words he ever penned were a little four-line poem that went like this:

> He drew a circle that shut me out—
> Heretic, rebel, a thing to flout.
> But Love and I had a wit to win:
> We drew a circle that took him in![12]

That should be the theme song of every encourager. If sung often enough by enough people, it will move our entire world toward excellence.

An Encourager's "Do" List

So how can we be encouragers to others? The following practices should be on the "do" list of every encourager.

1. *Be careful not to say a discouraging, critical word about others.* During the Civil War, General Whiting was jealous of General Robert E. Lee and consequently spread many rumors about him. The time came when General Lee had a chance to settle the score. President Jefferson Davis was considering Whiting for a key promotion. He wanted to know what General Lee thought of General Whiting. Without hesitation, Lee commended Whiting in the highest manner. Every officer present was astonished. One of them asked Lee after the interview if he had forgotten all the unkind words Whiting had spread about him. Lee responded, "I understand that the president wanted to know my opinion of Whiting, not Whiting's opinion of me."

2. *Do not withhold good from those to whom it is due.*

Simply being careful not to speak a discouraging, critical word about others is the place to start. Encouragement goes beyond that. Encouragement is not merely negative but positive. We must not only refrain from doing bad, but we must also refrain from holding back the good.

A wealthy woman was interviewing an applicant for a job on her household staff. "Do you know how to serve company?" she asked. "Yes, ma'am," the young lady replied. "I can serve them both ways." The matron queried, "What do you mean, 'both ways'?" The girl replied, "I can serve them so they will come back, and I can serve them so they won't come back. Both ways!"

There is only one way to serve other people. Do not hold back the good that is due them.

3. Then, this other suggestion: *Give them the good that is due them today.* Don't let good intentions replace encouraging actions. Write the letter now. Make the phone call now. Give the word of encouragement now. Lend the helping hand now. As the poet put it,

> Bring me all the flowers today,
>   Whether pink, or white or red;
> I'd rather have one blossom now
> Than a truckload when I'm dead.

AUTHOR UNKNOWN

Or, as another quip puts it, "An ounce of taffy now is worth more than a pound of 'epitaphy' later on."

The Clowns of Rome

Henri Nouwen, born and raised in Holland and ordained there as a Catholic priest, lived many years in the United States where his fame grew. His secret longing, however, was to spend some time in Rome and enjoy living in the shadow of the Vatican. Finally, his dream came true, and he moved to Rome. Rome impressed him with all of its splendor. However, Nouwen was most impressed by the unsung acts of service performed each day by people behind the scenes whom he called "the clowns of Rome." In describing the experience, Nouwen wrote, "I started to realize that in the great circus of Rome, full of lion tamers and trapeze artists whose dazzling feats claim our attention, the real and true story was told by the clowns."

Who were these "clowns of Rome"? Nouwen called them clowns because, like the funny men in the circus, they brought encouragement, laughter, and a release from the tension. These "peripheral people who by their humble, saintly lives evoke a smile and awaken hope" were not well known, nor did they boast much of their accomplishments. Rather, by their quiet dedication and service to others, they were at work in places terrorized by violence, immobilized by apathy, and enslaved by self-centered materialism. In such places they brought consolation, comfort, hope, encouragement, and a little humor when we are tempted to take life too seriously.[13]

Like Barnabas they are encouragers. Are they successful according to the standards of the world? No. But by their love, encouragement, and service they are standards of excellence for a world filled with people who seem to care only about themselves.

Points to Remember

If you simply focus on yourself, you will never experience excellence. So remember:

1. The debilitating effect of loneliness can be broken by a flow of love from your life into the lives of others.
2. In a world of critical words which tear people down, excellence comes through positive words that build people up.
3. Nothing builds self-worth like encouragement from others.
4. Discouraging words should be banished from our vocabulary.

5. Encouragement involves more than our words.
    It also involves our actions. We encourage
    not only by sharing our concern but also by
    helping others bear their burdens.
6. Encouragement needs to be given out on a
    daily basis.

Excellence comes when individuals extend the circle of their
love to others and become encouragers of one another.

10
He Threw It Out of Bounds

It was the fall of 1973. The scene was Waco, Texas. The setting was Baylor Stadium. On homecoming weekend, alumni returned from all over the country to watch the Bears play football. Grant Teaff's Baylor Bears had begun the year with great expectations. However, the opening season loss to Oklahoma was only a harbinger of things to come. Midway into the season, on homecoming day, facing the Texas Christian University Horned Frogs, Baylor was trying to win their first conference game for the year.

The game reflected the season. Baylor played dismally. With about eleven minutes left in the game, TCU led by 34-7. Suddenly, Baylor came alive. Led by Neal Jeffrey, the Bear offense staged an incredible comeback. They scored three quick touchdowns. With two minutes left in the game, TCU led by only 34-28.

Baylor stopped TCU, received the punt, and was on the move again. First down on the TCU fifteen-yard line! Neal Jeffrey tossed a screen pass to Gary Lacy for a nine-yard gain. Second and one on the TCU six. TCU threw Baylor for a four-yard loss on the next play. With the ball on the ten, Baylor faced a third and five situation. Time out was called by Baylor, their last time out. With forty-three seconds to go, third down and five yards to go for a first, Neal Jeffrey conferred with Coach Teaff on the sidelines. The play was called. As Jeffrey trotted back toward the huddle, Teaff yelled, "If your receiver is covered, throw it away."

Jeffrey barked the signals, and the ball was snapped. The wide receivers were covered. Then, Jeffrey spotted the tailback flaring out from the backfield. Jeffrey laid the ball out to him. From out of nowhere the defender flashed and stuck the receiver for a three-yard loss. Now Baylor faced a fourth and eight. No time outs. What would Jeffrey do?

The Baylor quarterback rushed the team to the huddle, brought them quickly to the line, took the snap, and stepped back from the line of scrimmage. Then, he threw the ball out of bounds to stop the clock. Neal Jeffrey forgot that it was fourth down. The ball went over to TCU. The game was lost.

Fourth down, no time outs, the game clock running out, thirteen yards from victory. And he threw it out of bounds! One word flashed through Neal Jeffrey's mind as he came to the sideline, sobbing in disappointment: *failure!* That's what he thought of himself: *failure!* If that was the end of the story, perhaps the word would have forever tagged the career of Neal Jeffrey.

That was not the end of the story. That was instead the beginning of the most dramatic story in Baylor football history. In 1974, the next season, for the first time in fifty years, Baylor won the Southwest Conference Championship. Time after time they came from behind to win the game. Time after time the Bears arose from the threshold of defeat and surged to victory. How were they able to do that? Ask any member of that team, and he will point back to that game in the fall of 1973 when they experienced the agony of defeat. What transformed losers into champions was their unwillingness to be defeated by their failure.[1]

Have you ever been in that spot? Fourth down, no time outs, time running out, and you blew it? All of us have known the agony of defeat. The truth that transforms apparent failures into eventual successes is the conviction that no failure need be final. The failures of your life can be the seedbeds out of which victory blossoms.

So here is the principle:

LEARN TO MOVE PAST YOUR FAILURES

A Failure That Wasn't Final

Not many young men had the opportunities which came to John Mark. The city was where the action was, and that is where John Mark lived. The political maneuvering and the social manipulating which characterized the city were part and parcel of his life. Even more important, John Mark experienced first hand the most significant religious development in centuries. Like every Jewish lad, John Mark looked forward to the promised Messiah of God. Suddenly, a man appeared who stirred the long-dormant hopes of Israel with the possibility that He was the Messiah. His name was Jesus. For three years He traveled the countryside, teaching with perception and healing with power. The common people loved this Jesus. The religious rulers hated Him. This festering hatred led finally to a plot to remove Jesus from the scene. The plot culminated in Jesus' final trip to Jerusalem.

Imagine the excitement of John Mark when he learned that Jesus and His disciples would take the Passover in John Mark's house. The impressions of that night as he watched Jesus and His friends never left him, not for the rest of his life.

Jesus led His friends out to Gethsemane's garden where He often retired for solace. The events then moved with such frightening speed John Mark could not put it all together. Jesus was arrested, tried, taken to Golgotha, and put to death. That was a Friday he would never forget.

Then, on Sunday the word came to him that Jesus had arisen from the dead. Some reported that Jesus wanted the disciples to go to Jerusalem and wait. Wait for what? None of them knew for sure. But to Jerusalem they went, to John Mark's house, and they waited. There the Holy Spirit came in a new manifestation. With the power of the Holy Spirit, the disciples moved out into Jerusalem. The Christian church was launched.

Here's the picture. John Mark had deep roots in the faith. He had every advantage. He had been exposed to the essentials of Christianity; he was no newcomer to the scene but instead one whose entire life had been lived under the shadow of Christianity.

It is no surprise, then, that when Paul and Barnabas set out on their first missionary journey, they decided to take John Mark with them. The surprise is what happened midway through the journey.

He Failed Man and God

Paul, Barnabas, Mark, and company had just finished the first leg of their trip. Their mission venture in Cyprus had been a tremendous success. Now, the missionary band moved into Perga in Pamphylia. That's where Mark's problem surfaced. He reached the point where he said, "God, I'm through. I'm not going to go any further. I quit." Mark checked out on God and went home.[2] Chapter one in Mark's story can be entitled "The Failure."

Why did this young man with so much going for him turn from his task and go home? Why did he fail?

Perhaps his *situation* provoked the action. Mark was a long way from home. The road the mission party was to travel frightened Mark. The circumstances were unpleasant. He thought about the unknown land toward which they were headed, the hard ground upon which they would have to sleep, the gangs of robbers hiding in the narrow mountain passes, and he didn't want to go. Perhaps Mark quit because he didn't like the circumstances in which he would have to carry out his ministry.

Failure often us from that source. We are stymied by the circumstances of our lives. Our surroundings hold too many threats. The way forward is too shrouded in darkness and uncertainty. So we quit.

Perhaps Mark gave up and headed back home because of *satisfaction*. Mark might have thought he had done enough. After all, he had been a part of the successful work in Cyprus. Many lives had been changed. He was thankful for what had happened, but he had other plans on his agenda. Satisfied with what he had done, he went back home.

One of the most perplexing factors about people is that so many of them start off like rockets, and then they fizzle. Why does that happen? Primarily because people come to the point where they feel they have done enough. They are satisfied with their relationship with God, satisfied with what they have accomplished, and satisfied with what they have done. They have done enough, so they quit.

Another suggestion about Mark's failure is that *spite* was the key factor. As the story unfolds in the Book of Acts, a subtle change appears. Initially, the biblical writer spoke of "Barnabas and Saul [Paul]" (Acts 13:2). Shortly, he began to talk about "Paul and Barnabas" (Acts 13:43). Why the change? Evidently, Paul took over leadership of the mission venture. That was the problem. Mark, you see, was the nephew of Barnabas. Maybe he became disenchanted with the takeover by Paul. Perhaps in anger, he left the group.

Does that happen to people today? You bet it does. Someone hurts our feelings, and we quit. Someone is given a more important position in the organization, and we get mad. Someone else receives more praise than we do, and we burn on the inside. Finally the slow burn erupts, "If that's the way they are going to be, they can have it. Nobody appreciates me anyway. So I quit."

Failure comes for many reasons. Perhaps all three were at work in Mark's life. This much we know: Mark had a chance to accomplish something significant, and he quit. Thus ends the first chapter of his life.

The Comeback

However, that was not the end of the story. Chapter 2 of Mark's story has a different ending. Let me describe the scenes of this final chapter.

The first scene in chapter 2 of Mark's life came when Paul and Barnabas prepared to go on a second mission venture. When Barnabas insisted on taking John Mark along, Paul and Barnabas split. Paul took Silas as his partner. Barnabas took John Mark to Cyprus. John Mark had returned to the work.[3]

Scene two revealed a reconciliation between John Mark and Paul. The impact of this reconciliation was reflected in Paul's desire, near the end of his life, to have John Mark with him.[4]

Scene three focused on a book, written by this same Mark, which for two thousand years has powerfully proclaimed the gospel story. The book is called the Gospel of Mark. John Mark was the author.

The first chapter in Mark's life told of a young man who quit on God, but that was not the end of the story. The final chapter showed a man who had been regained for God's cause. The weak had become strong. The deserter had become dedicated. The failure was transformed into success. Mark refused to be defeated by his failure.

Life's Closed Doors

What do you do when faced by a closed door in life? A young boy from Missouri named Harry had to answer that question. He gave evidence of brilliance on the piano even as a child. In addition to being gifted, Harry had such discipline that at the age of seven he was at the keyboard by five each morning. He practiced faithfully for hours each day. Under the tutelage of Mrs. E. C. White, he produced each day stronger hope that he would eventually reach greatness.

When Harry was fifteen, Mrs. White brought news to her star pupil. Paderewski, the greatest pianist of the day, was coming to town. The young boy was thrilled as he listened to Paderewski play. Mrs. White took her pupil backstage after the concert to meet Paderewski. With trembling voice, the young boy told the world-renowned pianist that he played his minuet. "There is a part of it," young Harry explained, "that I do not know how to execute." Paderewski walked back with the boy to the empty stage and to the piano. The boy sat at the same piano where Paderewski had played only a few minutes before. As the student played, Paderewski gave a smile of approval to his teacher. A bright future seemed to loom before him.

Then ensued the closed door. The next year Harry's father lost everything in the Kansas City grain market. Harry had to go to work, and his dreams of the concert stage were shattered.

Did the boy give up on life? Did he let this closed door stop him?

Not at all, for this young, gifted, promising pianist would become world famous before his life was over, as president of the United States. His name was Harry S. Truman.[5]

The Man Who Made the Future

The biography of Thomas Alva Edison is entitled: *The Man Who Made the Future.* That label, although correct, was not easily attained. Many closed doors met him in his long and illustrious career. The primary closed door, at the beginning of his life, was his deafness. Since Edison could still converse with people, his condition could more accurately be defined as hardness of hearing. Nevertheless, this closed door could have been a barrier to his development. Instead, he turned it into an advantage.

The isolation caused by his deafness drove Thomas to find consolation in the Detroit library. Here he would start with the first book on the bottom shelf and work his way along until that shelf was finished. Then, he would start on the next one. A closed door of hardness of hearing was turned into an open door of hunger for books.

How could a hard-of-hearing man compete in the world so dominated by sound? Again, Edison turned a closed door into an open door, even during his early days as a telegraph operator. He later recalled, "While I could hear unerringly the loud ticking of the instrument, I could not hear other and perhaps distracting sounds. I could not even hear the instrument of the man next to me in a big office."

The closed door again became an open door in the development of the telephone. Edison explained that his difficulty in hearing the faint sounds of the early telephone convinced him of the need for improvements. The result was the all-important carbon transmitter which was essential for the further development of the telephone.

As for the gramophone, Edison was certain that his deafness was his primary asset. He declared, "Deafness, pure and simple, was responsible for the experimentation which perfected the machine. It took me twenty years to make a perfect record of piano music because it is full of overtones. I now can do it—just because I'm deaf." A closed door became an open door.

Edison's biographer pointed out another advantage of his hardness of hearing. Since he was hard of hearing, Edison always demanded that agreements be made in writing. This practice saved him many times in an era notorious for financial swindle.

Edison's deafness could have been a closed door that prevented this brilliant man from achieving excellence. Instead, he transformed his closed door into an open door that enabled him to become "the man who made the future."[6]

A Continuing Story

History is replete with examples of that same dynamic truth. That was not just Mark's story, and Harry Truman's story, and Thomas Alva Edison's story. That has been the story of many individuals across the ages.

John Creasy was an author who received 743 rejection slips on manuscripts sent to publishers. He was a failure of the worst kind. He moved passed those failures, however, to become the author of 560 books that sold over sixty million copies. No failure need be final.

Albert Einstein was thought to be retarded by his parents. He did so poorly in high school in every subject except math that his teachers advised him to drop out of school. They predicted he would never amount to anything. He was a failure. He moved past that failure, however, to discover and define the law of relativity. No failure need be final.

Phillips Brooks became a teacher in Boston Latin School, a position for which he seemed preeminently qualified. He lasted only a few months. His headmaster commented that Phillips "had in him no single element of a successful school teacher" and set Phillips packing with the conclusion that he had never known a man who failed as a schoolmaster to succeed in any other occupation. He had failed at the age of twenty. Phillips Brooks overcame that failure, however, to become one of the finest pulpiteers in all of American history. No failure need be final.[7]

What to Do with Your Failure

Have you failed at something? Have you failed in your responsibilities as a father or a husband? Have you failed in your responsibilities as a mother or a wife? Have you failed in your work? Have you failed in school? Have you failed in some interpersonal relationship? Have you failed in some area of your life? If so, join the crowd. We have all failed at something.

What should we do with our failure?

1. The first step is to *learn from it.* What caused the failure? Was it something you did? Was it an unhealthy attitude you displayed? Was it lack of preparation or effort? Was the challenge something for which you were not skilled?

Edison consoled a colleague who was lamenting that thousands of experiments on a certain project had failed to discover anything. Edison explained, "I cheerily assured him that we had learned something, for we had learned for a certainty that the thing couldn't be done that way, and that we would have to try some other way."[8] Go to school with your failure and learn from it.

2. Then, *let go of it.* After you have learned the lessons that failure needs to teach you, let go of it. Don't invite the failure to live with you permanently. Accept the fact that the failure is behind you, and present that failure to a God who is big enough to help you move past it. Then release it.

A talented, young black girl made her debut at New York's Town Hall, but she was not ready for it. Consequently, the critics flailed her. She returned to Philadelphia in disgrace. Part of her early support had come from a special fund provided by members of her church. This "Fund for Marian Anderson's Future" had launched her career. Now she returned in failure.

Marian's embarrassment and depression lasted for more than a year. Through that time, her mother continued to encourage her. Finally, one of the motherly pep talks sank in. She told her daughter, "Marian, grace must come before greatness." Motivated by those words, Marian Anderson went on to a distinguished career during which she also helped many others discouraged by their first failures.[9]

Failure came. But when Marian Anderson was able to release her failure, then she was ready to move forward.

3. The third step is to *live above your failure*. An ancient German proverb suggests that each person must carve his life out of the wood he has. The wood of life includes our failures as well as our successes, our burdens as well as our blessings. When we take the broad view of our life, we realize that failure is simply one ingredient out of many. Put in its proper perspective, failure no longer appears as threatening. We know we can live above it.

Frank Laubach learned to live above his failure. At forty-five, missionary Frank Laubach was a theological seminary professor in the Philippines. He was next in line for president of the seminary. However, the board selected someone else. Laubach took off for the hills to sulk. He was angry about the unfairness of life and God's seeming lack of justice. He was a failure in his own eyes.

Was that the end of his story? Not on your life. Frank developed in his solitude a technique for teaching hundreds of millions of people throughout the world to read for the first time. He became the father of the modern literacy movement. A failure, Frank Laubach learned to live above that failure and on that new level, he found how to achieve excellence.[10]

Messed It Up So Bad No One Can Play It

Casey Stengel was still managing baseball when most men of his age were sitting back in their easy chairs admiring their trophies. The unique spirit he brought to the game of baseball has been permanent in its impact.

One day he was hitting some balls to a rookie in right field who missed every fly ball. Then Casey hit some on the ground, and he missed those too. Casey called him in from the field and advised, "I want to show you how it is done. You hit some balls to me." The rookie lofted a few fly balls to Stengel who also missed every one of them. Then the rookie hit some grounders, and Stengel missed those, too. Stengel jogged in and chided the young player, "You messed up right field so bad nobody can play it!"

That is not true of your life. No failure has messed up your life so bad that you cannot still play it, for no failure need be final.

Points to Remember

Failure often appears on the road toward excellence. So remember:

1. Neither proper background nor strong desire will prevent failure from coming to your life.
2. The cause of failure is varied. Unpleasant circumstances, satisfaction with what we have done, and a vengeful spirit toward others can lead to failure.
3. When the closed doors come in life, do not focus on them. Instead, look around for an alternate door which may be open.
4. Failure in one area of life does not mean you are a failure. It may mean that the task was wrong for you at that point.
5. Face each failure with the question, "What can I learn from this experience?"
6. Once you have acknowledged your failure and learned its lessons, release it.
7. Failure can be a platform for future achievement.

Excellence comes to those who are able to move past their failure.

11
Face-to-Face
with a Christian Bear

Jim had everything: money, popularity, political clout in his community, and a reputation as a man of peerless character. He had everything except one thing—a stuffed grizzly bear for the phenomenal game room in his house. One day Jim decided he would fulfill his dream. He made plans, set out for his destination, and arrived with the anticipation that he would soon capture his prize.

He sensed that he was getting close. The hair standing on the back of his neck gave the clue. Sure enough, as Jim turned the corner on a narrow, winding path up the side of a mountain, he found himself face-to-face with the biggest grizzly bear he had ever seen. Calm and cool, Jim raised his gun. Before he could pull the trigger, his foot slipped. The gun went flying as he fell off the side of the cliff, managing to save himself by catching the edge of the cliff with the tips of his fingers. Scrambling back up to the trail, he was in a real predicament, for the grizzly bear attacked.

Jim turned and started running down the hill as fast as he could, the bear in hot pursuit. As he neared the bottom of the mountain, he slipped again, this time tumbling head over heels through the short grass. He ended up on his knees.

In addition to being rich, brave, and astute, Jim was also religious. Realizing he was on his knees and a grizzly bear was on his trail, he thought this would be a good time to pray. He bowed his head, held his hands together, and began to pray. "Oh, Lord," he cried, "let this be a Christian bear."

When Jim opened his eyes, he realized that the bear was kneeling beside him, head bowed, hands folded in prayer. "Praise the Lord," Jim cried exultantly. "It is a Christian bear."

Suddenly, he realized what the bear was praying. "Lord, bless this food I am about to eat to the nourishment of my body!" It was a Christian bear, but it was still a bear.[1]

Sometimes we find ourselves in a situation like that, facing foes which are all around us. At times the challenges before us seem difficult. At other times, they seem impossible to meet. The good news is that we don't have to reach our goals or face our challenges or overcome our difficulties or achieve excellence alone. Divine help is available.

So here is the tenth principle for experiencing excellence:

BRING GOD INTO THE SITUATION THROUGH PRAYER

A Mount Sinai of a Man

One scholar calls him "a Mount Sinai of a man with a heart like a thunderstorm."[2] Another calls him "the grandest and most romantic character Israel ever produced."[3] By another he is referred to as "the Martin Luther of Old-time Israel."[4] His name was Elijah, and he erupted onto the scene of ancient Israel with volcanic suddenness during the reign of King Ahab. Ahab, under Jezebel's influence, was leading Israel away from God. Elijah desired to turn Israel back to God.

In the roll call of Old Testament heroes, Elijah is near the top of the list. Wrote one scholar, "There were two sorts of prophets, prophets of deeds and prophets of words. Of the latter the greatest is doubtless Isaiah. Of the former there has not been among men a greater than Elijah."[5]

What was the secret to his success? What was the key to the excellence Elijah achieved? The key to his life was not his courage, but rather his courage grew out of this key. The key was not his character, but instead his character was refined by this key. The key was not his consistency. On the contrary, his consistency was made possible by this key. The key to Elijah's life, the reason for his preeminence, the source of his courage, character, and consistency is that at each point of his life, Elijah brought God into the situation through prayer. The practice that provided power for the prophet was prayer.

The Scenes of Elijah's Life

Elijah's ministry can be divided into five scenes:

In scene one, before King Ahab, when confronted by *danger,* Elijah brought God into the situation through prayer.[6]

In scene two, by the brook Cherith, when confronted by *deficiency,* Elijah brought God into the situation through prayer.[7]

In scene three, at Zarephath, when confronted by a *detour,* Elijah brought God into the situation through prayer.[8]

In scene four, on Mount Carmel, confronted with the *defiance* of the prophets of Baal and Asherah, Elijah again brought God into the situation through prayer.[9]

In scene five, in the wilderness, when confronted by *discouragement,* Elijah once more brought God into the situation through prayer.[10]

In every situation, confronted by every circumstance, Elijah's response was always the same. He realized that he could not face his problems in his own strength. He realized further that he did not have to. So in each scene of his life, Elijah brought God into it through prayer.

Dealing with Danger

Few of us have known personally the danger that engulfed the lives of the Americans held hostage in Tehran for over 400 days. They faced constant danger, and the threat of death was always hanging over their heads. How did they face this danger?

Bruce Laingen, ranking American hostage, shared his personal testimony with the members of his church shortly after his return. He testified there was no hostage he knew of who failed to draw on religious strength during the long ordeal. In solitary confinement, during a power shortage, with Iranian voices raised on the rooftops praising their god for some temporary military victory, Laingen admitted that he felt isolated. However, he testified that his "quiet nightly dialogues with my God" comforted him and enabled him to make it through.

What do you do when danger looms large before you? Jesus suggested that you have only two choices.[11] You can pray and in the power of that prayer stand firm. Or you can refuse to pray and as a result of that prayerlessness, lose heart.

When confronted by danger, whether in Tehran or in your hometown, the answer is prayer.

When Deficiencies Arise

What do you do when deficiencies sap the strength of your life? I'm not talking about those minor elements you can supply yourself but those monumental needs you cannot possibly provide on your own. What can you do about those deficiencies? You can stand impotent and immobilized like those to whom James spoke in his epistle, "You have not because you ask not."[12] Or, like the apostle Paul, you can forge forward in faith because you have talked to a God who will supply all your needs according to his riches in glory in Christ Jesus.[13]

Prayer during times of deficiency can be tinted with selfishness. Like the parrot who constantly blurted out, "Let us pray." At all hours of the day and night, he would repeat the same phrase, "Let us pray." His owner did not teach him the words, nor did he understand where the parrot learned them. But over and over again, the parrot would say, "Let us pray." On a trip, the man saw a beautiful female parrot. He decided that he would purchase her as a companion to his other parrot. When he put the new parrot into the cage, the other parrot blurted out, "My prayers have been answered!"

Although selfishness often creeps into our prayers, the fact nevertheless remains true. A part of prayer is to present our personal petitions to the Lord, asking for His supplies to make up for our deficiencies.

A newcomer to heaven was given a tour. He was curious about huge warehouses on each side of the road, so he asked the tour guide to take him inside one of them. The warehouse was lined with shelf after shelf, and on the shelves were bundles. Everywhere he looked he saw these bundles. "What are they?" he asked his guide. The guide explained, "These bundles are answered prayers which have never yet been asked for?"

Heaven is full of bundles which we have never received because we have not asked for them. When confronted by deficiencies, the solution is prayer.

Dealing with Detours

What do you do when a detour moves you off the main road onto a side street? You have two choices. You can drown yourself in despair, wailing, "Why did this happen to me?" Or you can place the detour before the Lord in prayer and ask, "What do You want to show me as we walk down this side road together?"

The year was 1920. The scene was the examining board for selecting missionaries. Standing before the board was a young man named Oswald Smith. One dream dominated his heart. He wanted to be a missionary. Over and over again, he prayed, "Lord, I want to go as a missionary for you. Open a door of service for me." Now, at last, his prayer would be answered.

When the examination was over, the board turned Oswald Smith down. He did not meet their qualifications. He failed the test. Oswald Smith had set his direction, but now life gave him a detour.

What would he do? As Oswald Smith prayed, God planted another idea in his heart. If he could not go as a missionary, he would build a church which could send out missionaries. And that is what he did. Oswald Smith pastored The People's Church in Toronto, Canada, which sent out more missionaries than any other church at that time. Oswald Smith brought God into the situation, and God transformed his detour into a main thoroughfare of service.[14]

Many times, either by choice or by circumstance, we will be

diverted onto a side road. When detours come, the answer is prayer.

When You Are in Conflict

Joe had a problem. He did not like his boss. Every day brewed another conflict between him and his boss. What to do? He discussed the matter with his friend who suggested that for thirty days he pray for his boss. Reluctantly, Joe agreed. After about ten days, Joe's boss stopped him in the hall with the question, "What's wrong with you? You're doing something different, and I can't figure out what it is?" Joe assured him it was nothing. About five days later, the boss sat down in Joe's office and demanded an answer. "Something has happened to you," he persisted. "You don't argue anymore. You get along. You're not bugging me. I want to know what's going on?" Joe explained, "I've been praying for you for the last fifteen days." The boss queried, "Why are you doing that?" Joe answered, "Because I don't like you." Joe thought perhaps he would get fired for that comment. Instead, the boss continued, "Well, let's sit down and talk about why you don't like me." That was the beginning of a new relationship with his boss.

What do you do when you face the defiance of evil men? How do you deal with opposition? You can fight them in your own strength and lose the battle, or, you can bring God into the situation through prayer and let Him win the victory.

Life is a daily struggle for most of us. Conflict often marks our day. When confronted by those who defy you, face them with prayer.

When Discouragement Sets In

How do you deal with your discouragement? What do you do when you feel like you are at the end of your rope? You can give up and let go of the rope. Or you can tie a knot in the end of the rope through prayer, and hold on until morning comes.

Depression is one of the most common emotions of life. Nathan Kline, director of the Research Center at the Rockland State

Hospital in New York, refers to depression as "the common cold of psychiatric ills."[15] The prophet Elijah experienced depression.[16] Because many factors are involved in causing depression, many factors are involved in the cure. However, this much becomes clear as we read Elijah's story. His cure began when he got in touch with God through prayer.

Discouragement comes because we are in some way frustrated by our inability to cope. Coping power comes from God. You get in touch with God through prayer. Therefore, when discouragement comes, you find your strength in prayer.

Slot-machine Praying

Two qualifications need to be mentioned at this point: one concerning the purpose of prayer and the other relating to the condition for prayer.

The proper *purpose* of prayer needs to be remembered. While all that I have said is true, that we need to pray when danger, deficiencies, detours, defiance, and discouragement come so that God will supply our needs, there is a higher level to prayer. Some practice slot-machine praying, that is, it won't cost too much, and I might hit the jackpot!

True prayer lives on a higher level. The purpose of prayer is not to enlist God on our agenda. The higher purpose is to submit ourselves to God's agenda. Prayer is not a tool to obtain something from God. Prayer is an opportunity to come into God's presence, to learn of Him, and to lock into His plan.

We must also remember the *condition* of prayer. Jesus placed this condition on prayer. He said, "If you abide in Me, and My words abide in you, ask whatever you wish, and it shall be done for you."[17] You cannot have the provision if you do not meet the condition.

James took the same position in his Epistle. He wrote, "The effective prayer of a righteous man can accomplish much."[18] You cannot have the power if you do not meet the condition.

Neither Jesus nor James meant that only a righteous person can pray, that only after years of righteous living can a person dare to come into God's presence. The privilege of prayer is available to every child of God. What they affirmed is that a direct connection exists between the spiritual condition of the life of the person who prays and the results of his prayer. One man has rightly concluded, "The most important single factor in effective prayer is that the person praying be in the right relationship with God."[19]

Understanding Prayer

How then can you pray? What is involved in prayer? You need to understand some basic things about prayer.

You need to understand the *whoever* of prayer. Any Christian can pray, for the good news of the New Testament is that through Jesus Christ we have been given access to the Father.[20]

In the Bible, people of all types prayed. In Psalm 34:6, a poor man prayed. In 1 Kings 9:3, a rich man prayed. In 1 Samuel 12:7, a married person prayed. In Luke 2:38, a widow prayed. In Acts 10:2, a military person prayed. In Acts 9:10, a civilian prayed. In Acts 7:55, a holy man prayed. In Jonah 2:1, a rebellious man prayed. In 1 Kings 3:1-13, a king prayed. In Luke 18:13, a publican prayed. Whoever wants to can come before God in prayer and fellowship with Him. The recognition of that fact is the first step in understanding prayer.

You need to understand the *whenever* of prayer. When should you pray? You should pray at all times. Christians who are most effective in their prayers have a particular place where they do most of their praying, and they withdraw to that place at a specific time. Fine. But never so emphasize the need for a certain time and place for prayer that you overlook the biblical injunction to pray at all times.

Paul admonished Christians to "pray without ceasing."[21] The Greek word Paul used was used in other manuscripts to describe a persistent cough. When you have a hacking, persistent cough, you are always either coughing or on the verge of a cough. So it should be with your prayers. Each moment of the day should find you in prayer or on the verge of a prayer. When you pray without ceasing, then you are beginning to understand prayer.

You need to understand the *wherever* of prayer. Where should you be when you pray? You can pray anywhere. The Bible presents a variety of pictures of men and women at prayer. In Daniel 9:20, Daniel prayed in jail. In Nehemiah 9:27, the Hebrews prayed for their captive brethren in a foreign land. In Exodus 17:9, Moses prayed in the midst of the battlefield. In Luke 23:42, the penitent thief prayed on the cross. In Jonah 2:1, the prophet prayed in the stomach of the great fish. The practice of praying everywhere is another step in the direction of understanding what prayer really is.

You need to understand the *whatever* of prayer. For what should you pray? You can pray to God about everything. The Old Testament historian tells of a time in Hezekiah's life when he received a threatening communication from Sennacherib, king of Assyria. It was the kind of news that would send a person into a series of sleepless nights. But Hezekiah spread the matter before the Lord in prayer.[22]

Whatever the invading anxiety is in your life, you can do that with it. You can go up before God and spread it out before Him. When blessing comes, you can thank God. When burdens come, you can seek God's assistance. When you have failed, you can ask for God's forgiveness. When you have succeeded, you can praise God for His help. When you are burdened for someone, you can intercede on that person's behalf. When you are burdened for yourself, you can send up your personal petitions. When you don't know what to do, you can ask God for His guidance. When you don't know what to say, you can wait for His Spirit to utter those words which cannot be spoken. You can pray to God about everything.

His Hand Was in the Chair

An old Scotsman was very ill. His minister went to see him. As he sat down by the sick man's bed, the minister noticed another chair drawn up by the other side of the bed. "Well, Donald," he said. "I see I am not your first visitor." The old man looked surprised. "I'm talking about the chair by your bed," the minister explained. "Looks like someone else has been here." The man said, "I want to tell you about that chair. Years ago I found it difficult to pray. One day I shared with my pastor. He told me not to worry about kneeling down. 'Just sit down,' he told me, 'put a chair opposite you, and imagine Jesus in it, and talk to Him as you would to a friend.' " The old Scotsman added, "I've been doing it ever since."

A while later the daughter of the sick man called for the minister. When he answered, the daughter told him how her father had died very suddenly. She had no idea death was near. "I had just gone to lie down for an hour or two, for he seemed to be sleeping so comfortably. When I went back to check on him, he was dead. He had not moved since I saw him before, except that his hand was on the empty chair at the side of his bed."[23]

You don't have to face life alone. You have a companion, the God who created the world and all that is in it. He can be your companion through life. Through companionship with Him you will receive the power to rise above the dilemmas and difficulties of life and experience excellence.

Points to Remember

Excellence is not a do-it-yourself project, nor do you lift yourself to excellence by the power of your own life. True excellence is possible only in a life of prayer. So remember:

1. The most productive spiritual lives have always been well grounded in prayer.
2. Prayer makes available to us the resources of God to help us deal with danger, deficiency, detours, defiance, and discouragement.
3. Prayer has a higher level. The primary aim of prayer is not to get things from God for our own purpose but to get in tune with God's purpose.
4. The context for effective prayer is a life which abides in Christ.

5. Any Christian can pray anytime at anyplace about anything.

6. Prayer produces peace, power, and purpose in the life of individual

Excellence comes to those who are willing to bring God into their lives through prayer.

12
Independence
or Interdependence

The guy was obviously depressed as he sat on the park bench. So forlorn looking was he that the policeman who patrolled the park sat down beside him to console him. "Something the matter?" asked the policeman of the young man who sat staring into space. "Yeah," he said, "you just wouldn't believe it. Two months ago my grandfather died and left me $85,000 and some oil wells." The policeman responded, "That doesn't sound like something to get upset about." "Yeah, but you haven't heard the whole story yet. Last month my uncle died, and he left me $150,000." The policeman shook his head. "I don't understand," he said. "Why are you sitting here looking so unhappy?" The guy responded, "This month, so far, not a cent."

Some people are like that. They think the world owes them a living, and they make a career out of letting others take care of them. They are leeches who live off of the blood they drain from the lives of others.

At the opposite end of the spectrum are those who declare their independence from everyone. Like William Ernest Henley in the often-quoted "Invictus" they declare,

> It matters not how strait the gate,
> How charged with punishment the scroll
> I am the master of my fate;
> I am the captain of my soul.[1]

Living under the false assumption that they are islands of achievement completely separated from everyone else, some make a fetish of their independence.

Somewhere between the person who thinks everyone owes him a living and the person who doesn't think he owes anyone anything is the middle ground where a life of excellence is to be lived. So here is the eleventh principle in achieving excellence:

> REMEMBER THAT LIFE IS A TEAM SPORT

Sharing the Load

What a leader Moses was! Who else would have walked up before the pharoah, probably the most powerful man in the world at that time, and demanded, "Let these people go free?" Who else had such an encounter with God as Moses did on Mount Sinai? Who else could have molded that group of ex-slaves into a mighty army for God?

That does not, however, tell all the story. Study the life of Moses as he began his leadership over the liberated people, and you will discover that he did not stand alone. On one occasion, the people lined up before him to receive his judgment on matters great and small. They stood in line before him from morning until night. Moses' father-in-law Jethro, after watching the proceedings, suggested to the great Hebrew leader: "This is not going to work. You cannot do it alone. You need some help." So Jethro recommended to Moses that he select some able leaders who loved God and stood for the truth and appoint them as leaders over groups of thousands, and over groups of hundreds, and over groups of fifties, and over groups of tens.[2]

Why? Because Jethro knew that Moses could accomplish more in relationship with others than he could alone.

Holding Up His Arms

Moses was not only a dynamic political leader, he was also a military leader. As the Hebrews moved across the wilderness toward their Promised Land, many foes stood in their way. Perhaps the most formidable foe was the Amalekites. The forces of Moses and those of Amalek met on the plain of Rephidim. What was the result of the battle? The Hebrews wiped out the Amalekites. What a military leader Moses was!

That was not, however, all of the story. Moses did not personally lead the armies into the field. Joshua was the field general. Instead, Moses stood on a high point with the staff of God raised high over his head as a symbol of power. As long as he held his hands up, the Hebrews prevailed. But as soon as he let his hands down, Amalek prevailed. As the battle continued, Moses' hands became heavy. He could no longer hold them up on his own. So Aaron held up one hand, and Hur held up the other hand. With Moses' hands raising high the staff of God, Israel won the victory.[3]

What does this mean for us? The victory of Israel came not only because of Moses. Joshua, Hur, Aaron, and Moses combined their efforts. God used their united effort to win the victory. Together they were able to accomplish what alone Moses could not have done.

The Council of Mighty Men

Equal in power and fame to the name of Moses is the name of David. David was described as "a man after God's own heart."[4] Even as a young man, his fame eclipsed that of King Saul, for the women sang in the streets, "Saul has killed his thousands, but David has killed his tens of thousands."[5] He was the greatest military leader Israel ever had. He was the model after which Hebrew hopes for a Messiah were patterned. One cannot consider the story of David without marveling at the glorious achievements he made.

That does not, however, tell all the story. In the concluding chapters about David in 2 Samuel, we read of David's mighty men.[6] Thirty-three men are cited by name, with a summary of some of their activities which supported King David. The first three men are cited as being in the inner circle of David's friends. What does this mean? It is the reminder that David did not achieve his goals alone but in a fabric of relationships that enabled them to do together what David could not have accomplished alone.

Stuck with Three Friends

Buddy went to see a counselor. He was not satisfied with his life. He had problems and needed help. As the session closed, the counselor told Buddy to make three new friends that week and see what would happen. The next week, Buddy returned for another session. The counselor asked him how his week went. "Terrible," he replied "I made three new friends—and nothing happened. Now I'm stuck with three new friends."

If you have three genuine friends, then you are stuck with something very important. Because those friends will provide a framework of relationships which will enable you to achieve things you could never have achieved on your own.

Charles Kingsley once was asked, "What is the secret of your life?" He answered, "I had a friend."[7] He had discovered the importance of relationships.

Studies at the Carnegie Institute of Technology underscore the importance of relationships. In the field of engineering, for instance, the studies show that about 15 percent of one's financial success is due to technical knowledge and about 85 percent is due to skill in human engineering, that is, the ability to lead people and relate to them.

Dr. William Menninger discovered that when people are discharged from their jobs in industry, social incompetence accounted for 60 to 80 percent of the failures. Only 20 to 40 percent of the dismissals were due to technical incompetence.[8]

In our narcissistic age, we are continually encouraged to look out for number one, to put self first, to seek self-fulfillment and, if necessary, to win by intimidation. The trend of our day exalts the individual who stands alone against the world.

The truth is, we are all debtors to other people. One person put it like this: "Every person in the world is, in reality, a collective noun, encompassing the labor, interests, and involvements of a host of others."[9]

The Horsemen and the Mules

When Knute Rockne coached at Notre Dame, his running backs who absolutely pulverized the opposition were dubbed "The Four Horsemen." They ran roughshod over the opposition, and the sportswriters were exuberant in their praise and adulation.

Rockne, master psychologist that he was, noticed something happening to the team. So in one of the games, he held out the first-team linemen whom one sportswriter had humorously dubbed, "The Seven Mules." Now, the Four Horsemen were running behind the second-team linemen, and things didn't go too well. Notre Dame was pushed around in the first half.

Rockne came into the locker room at halftime to find the Four Horsemen dejectedly sitting in the corner. He asked "What's the matter, boys? Didn't you show them your press clippings?" In the second half, with the Seven Mules back in harness, the Four Horsemen learned why they had been so successful.[10]

What are running backs in football without linemen to block for them? They are the same as we would be without the support groups which tie into our lives in the different arenas where we work and live. Our interdependence with those around us should lead to gratitude in our lives. The gratitude is often missing.

A man walked into the post office one day and purchased a card. He turned to the man next to him and requested, "Sir, would you mind addressing this card for me?" The man, thinking the poor fellow could not write, gladly helped him out. When he handed the card back, the man needed another favor. "I hate to bother you again," he continued, "but would you mind writing a short message on the card for me?" The kind gentleman agreed to this second request and wrote out the message as the man dictated it to him. He gave the completed card to the man who looked at it for a moment and then asked one more favor. "I know this is an imposition, but would you mind doing one more thing for me? At the end of the message, would you apologize for the horrible handwriting?"

That kind of ingratitude is no more astounding than for a person to evaluate the achievement of his life with the simple statement, "Look what I have done." Before all of us are those who have laid the groundwork. Around all of us are those who have provided the support. Behind all of us are those who have nurtured us to the place where we are now. Therefore, the only proper response to the fact of our interdependence is gratitude.

Somebody Will Be Here

How can we express that gratitude? We are given a hint in an interesting story of a man on vacation with his son's family at a rented cottage on the New England seashore. On the first day of his vacation, he was out in the yard digging a hole. He was putting out a small plant. As the son observed the strenuous work of his dad, he asked him why he was going to such effort to put out a plant when this was not even their cottage. The son explained, "We won't even be at this cottage the next year." The father replied, "*Somebody* will be here."

That statement caught the son's attention, so he paused and watched for a moment. "What kind of plant is that?" he asked. "A century plant." "A century plant? You mean it won't bloom for a hundred years?" "Not that long," the father explained, "Maybe twenty or thirty years." The boy was astonished. "Why in the world would you come out on this hot morning on your vacation in a rented cottage to put out a plant that won't even bloom for twenty years?" The father paused and looked up at his son. "I saw one the other day, and realized that someone twenty or thirty years ago wanted to share it with me. And so he planted it for my enjoyment. *Some day,* I said to myself, *I'm going to plant one so that people will enjoy it after I'm gone.* And that's what I'm doing this morning."[11]

Self-centeredness says, "I'll do whatever brings pleasure to me." Mediocrity says, "I'll do just enough to get by." Excellence says, "I'll plant something which can be enjoyed by those who follow."

Others before us have contributed to our lives. Recognition of that truth will motivate us to contribute to the lives of those who come after us.

Our National Debt

As Americans, we are also interdependent with other nations. We often imply that we Americans are responsible for everything of value and worth in the world. The truth is, we are debtors to other nations for much of what we enjoy and hold dear today.

A typical American wakes up in the morning, garbed in pajamas, a garment of East Indian origin, and quickly looks at the clock, a medieval European invention. He rushes to the bathroom to shave, a rite developed by the priests of Egypt, and looks into a glass also invented by the Egyptians. He washes with soap, invented by the ancient Gauls, and dries himself with a Turkish towel. He pulls on clothes, many of which are from Japan and Australia, and fastens them with buttons which first appeared in Europe. He puts his feet into leather tanned in Argentina and ties about his neck a strip of colored cloth, which is a survival of the shoulder shawls worn by the seventeenth-century Croats.

When he goes to breakfast, before him in pottery vessels known as china is an orange, domesticated around the Mediterranean, a cup of coffee from Brazil, and waffles originally served in Scandinavia.

After breakfast, he reaches for a piece of molded felt, invented by the nomads of Eastern Asia, that we call a briefcase. If he lives in the big city, he takes his interurban train to work, an English invention.

He buys a newspaper with coins invented in ancient Libya and reads the news in letter characters invented by the Semites and provided for him by a printing process invented in Germany on paper material invented in China.

As he scans the terrible news of foreign lands, he gives utterances of fervent thanks to a Hebrew God in language borrowed from England that he is "100 percent (decimal system coming from the Greeks) independent American," the word *American* taken from Amerigo Vespucci, an Italian geographer.[12]

Who are we trying to kid? Why, the same people we try to kid when we claim we are "self-made individuals," completely independent of any outside influence, support, or help. No one ever achieves excellence without the help of others.

Making Friends and Enjoying People

The key, then, to achieving excellence in life is not making friends and influencing people. The key is making friends and enjoying people, for it is out of a framework of friendship that excellence arises.

Alan Loy McGinnis, in his classic book *The Friendship Factor,* pointed out five ways to deepen your relationship with other people.[13]

The place to begin is to *assign top priority to your relationships.* To those who enjoy life to its fullest, companions are very important. They spend time and expend effort developing those relationships. On the other hand, lonely people are often those who put little emphasis on cultivating friends. Ask yourself the question: "Is it important to me to develop intimacy in my relationships with others?" If the answer is yes, then you are ready for the second step.

People who develop close personal friends have learned how to *cultivate transparency.* McGinnis explained, "People with deep and lasting friendships may be introverts, extroverts, young, old, dull, intelligent, homely, good-looking; but the one characteristic they always have in common is openness. They have a certain transparency, allowing people to see what is in their hearts."[14] To develop friendships you have to be willing to become vulnerable to others. Let down the barriers. Open some doors. Remove some masks. Establish some bridges between your life and others.

The third step in developing friendships is to *talk about your affection.* An eskimo said to his girl friend, "I would drive my dogs a thousand miles to say, 'I love you.' " She responded, "That's a lot of mush!" That's usually our reaction to displays of emotion.

Men in particular are supposed to keep their emotions in check. Friendships, however, are not developed strictly on the rational level. Friendships are developed on the feeling level. Feelings of affection clearly and publicly declared are the framework of relationships.

To develop friendships we must also *learn the gestures of love.* Harry and Hilda were sitting quietly in the den. Hilda kept glancing at Harry out of the corner of her eye. Finally, she inquired, "Harry, you don't ever tell me you love me anymore." Harry put his paper down and responded, "I told you once when we got married. If I ever change my mind, I'll let you know!" That is not adequate in either marriage or friendships. Love is not just a feeling. Love is something you do. For friendships to be developed, you must learn how to express your affection and verbalize your feelings for other people.

McGinnis mentions a final step. Friendships are developed as you *create space in your relationships.* Possessiveness does not promote real intimacy. Rather, by encouraging your friend to develop his uniqueness, by allowing time for solitude, by encouraging him to develop other relationships as well, you create an atmosphere in which true intimacy can be developed.

Three Stages of Understanding

A young pastor, ready to work in his first church, approached a retired pastor for some insight into the challenging task ahead of him. He asked the wise minister to explain his concept of the ministry. What was it like to pastor a church? The retired pastor responded that he had actually gone through three different phases in his understanding.

In the first phase, as a young hotshot preacher recently out of seminary who thought more highly of himself than he should, he pictured the ministry like this: "The people of my congregation were out in the deep water, going down for the third time. I was high and dry on the shore, telling them how to get from where they were to where I was."

"Then," he added, "my concept changed. After a few years in the ministry, I came to a new understanding. The people were still in the water. And they were still in trouble. But now, I was at the edge of the water, with one foot on dry land and the other out in the water with my hand stretched out toward them to help them get from where they were to where I was."

"After many more years, in the twilight of my ministry, I finally came to a clear understanding," he concluded. "Then I understood that I was in the water with the people. They were holding me up. And underneath us all were the everlasting arms of God."

That is a picture of us all, whether in the ministry or in another vocation. There are always others who hold us up, and under us all are the everlasting arms of God.

Points to Remember

Some wag has remarked that behind every successful man is a supportive wife and a mother-in-law in shock! That may be true of some. What is true of all is that our achievement is largely dependent upon the people with whom we relate in life. So remember:

1. Every great leader has a group of men and women who believe in him and support him.
2. Each of us is a collective noun encompassing the lives of many other people, past and present.
3. Achievement comes through cooperation.
4. Gratitude is the only proper response to the contributions of others to our lives.
5. Planting something to benefit future generations is one of the finest ways to express that gratitude.
6. What is true of individuals is true of our nation: we are debtors to others.

7. Developing a fabric of friendship in our lives
    will provide the context for achieving excel-
    lence.

Excellence comes to those who realize their relationship with
others.

13
Excellence in an Average World

The ophthalmologist had never seen anyone quite like Sammy. He was in for an eye examination because he felt like he needed glasses. The doctor seated him before the chart and said, "Put your right hand over your right eye." Sammy put his right hand on his temple, above his right eye. The doctor shook his head and said, "Let's try this. Put your left hand over your left eye." Again, Sammy put his hand on his temple, above the eye. The doctor thought for a moment and then devised a plan. He took a paper sack, put it over Sammy's head, and cut out two flaps for his eyes. He would lift each flap for him to see the chart, one eye at a time. When the doctor lifted up the first flap, he thought he noticed a tear in Sammy's eye. He lifted up the other flap, and sure enough he did see tears. He thought to himself, *I must have cut him when I was making the flaps.* So he quickly took the sack off Sammy's head and asked, "What is the matter?" Sammy explained, "I sorta wanted horn-rims!"

Many today sorta want excellence, but you have been scared off from the pursuit of excellence by those who decry the positive thinkers and condemn the desire for success as self-centered and even satanic. Consequently, the inner desire for excellence is thwarted.

Granted some of the positive thinkers tend to come off sounding self-centered. And some put too much focus on what *we* can do. And success is often too much in the forefront of attention. Those statements notwithstanding, striving for excellence in an average

world is not only an acceptable pursuit, it is also a biblical impera-
tive.

In the Old Testament, there is this statement: "Whatever your
hand finds to do, verily, do it with all your might."[1]

The New Testament parallel was written by the pen of the
apostle Paul. He said, "Whether, then, you eat or drink or whatever you do, do all to the glory of God.[2]

This book on excellence is not a catalog of the things we can
do in our own power but a portrait of what we can become
through God's power. The principle discussed in chapter 11 is the
foundation of everything we experience. When we bring God into
the circumstances of our life, through prayer, God's power is
available to us. Through God's power we are able to realize the
potential within us and experience excellence. That is not human-
ism. It is New Testament Christianity at its best.

Neither is this book on excellence a charge to pit yourself
against the world with the desire to win by intimidation. Excellence does not come in the life of a person who plants himself
against all others but in the life of a person who joins with all
others in a fabric of relationships.

Denis Waitley's book *Seeds of Greatness* was criticized at this
very point. Partly to clarify where he stood, Waitley wrote a
sequel: *The Double Win.* What is the double win? He gave this
simple and brief definition of the Double Win: "If I help you win,
I win, too."[3]

When your goal is to be *the* best, then you are playing by the
win-lose playbook. In order to be *the* best, others have to be less
than the best.

When your goal is to be *your* best, then you are playing by the
win-win playbook. You can be *your* best at the same time others
can be *their* best. There is no necessary conflict.

In *The Winner's Edge,* Waitley wrote, "The 'Win-Lose' playbook that suggests that there must be a loser for every winner, that
winning by intimidation is fashionable, is obsolete. The 'Win-Win'
playbook is the only one that can endure. 'Win-Win' means, 'If I
help you win, then I win too!' The real winners in life get what

they want by helping others get what they want. Independence has been replaced by interdependence. There are too many people, too few resources, and too delicate a balance between nature and technology to produce winners in isolation today."[4]

Should success be our goal? Not in the narrow definition of that word, for success is self-centered and win-lose oriented. Excellence should be our goal. Each of us should strive for excellence in every phase of our lives.

Can each of us be *the* best? Should we even try? No, for when we strive to be *the* best, comparison, intimidation, arrogance, and aggression dominate our character. Being *your* best should be the goal. Such excellence, where a person's practice matches his or her potential, is a rare achievement in today's world.

A Model of Excellence

I am writing this chapter as the heated war called "The NBA Playoff" began to end the season. Philadelphia was eliminated in the first round by the Milwaukee Bucks, and with Philadelphia's loss came the final appearance of a man known as "Dr. J." Julius Winfield Erving completed his sixteen-season career in professional basketball. What a model of excellence he is.

Just listing his accomplishments in professional basketball boggles the mind. He was only the third player in NBA history to score over 30,000 points. He played five years in the ABA and eleven in the NBA, and was an all-star every season. Without question, on the court, he was one of the greatest players of all time.

What made Julius Erving so unique was his conduct off the court. "Elegance" and "dignity" are the words the sportswriters used to describe this unique man, both on and off the court, as he made his final rounds as the doctor of hoop.

One player commented about him, "I've never heard anybody knock him or express jealousy. Never one negative word. I can't name you one other player who has that status."[5]

Near the end of his final season, *The Denver Post* conducted an informal poll of sportswriters and sportscasters across the country, trying to identify the "nicest" people in sports. Erving's name appeared on by far the largest number of ballots.[6]

One of the sportswriters giving the final tribute to this great player, concluded his article with this assessment: "The Doctor was a teacher, a professor; the Doctor was a gentleman and a scholar."[7]

Julius Irving developed his potential to its fullest. He recognized his dependence on others and treated them with respect. He committed himself to being *his* best and achieved it. That's what excellence is all about.

Will You Be One?

In geography class, the teacher asked the class what shape the earth was in. Nine-year-old Jeremy blurted out, "My Daddy says that the world is in the worst shape it has ever been in." And it is.

What the world needs now is men and women who will rise above the crowd with a commitment to excellence. Will you be one?

Epilogue

You only get one chance at life
Days of peace and days of strife
Challenges to face, jobs to do
Continuous pressure all the way through
Don't be like the rest
Meet the test
Be your best.

Begin with a vision of what's ahead
Of what you want before you're dead
Determine the steps along the way
Of what you want to accomplish each day
Don't be like the rest
Meet the test
Be your best.

Watch out for detours that you will face
They're always there to slow your pace
Temptations which lead to forbidden sod
Trials tempting you to give up on God
Don't be like the rest
Meet the test
Be your best.

Open your eyes so you can see
The person God wants you to be
See yourself as the winner you are
The vision itself will take you far

Don't be like the rest
Meet the test
Be your best.

Then get into action, the time is now
"I'll do it today" should be your vow
Say no to the emotion that we call fear
Determine the task and get into gear
Don't be like the rest
Meet the test
Be your best.

Get your goals clearly in view
Then discipline yourself in what you do
Allow good habits to shape your life
To keep you on target in the midst of strife
Don't be like the rest
Meet the test
Be your best.

Let go of your past, it's behind you now
It can't be recaptured anyhow
Today is the day that can be great
If you will learn how to concentrate
Don't be like the rest
Meet the test
Be your best.

Your mind is an asset that has no peer
Don't fill it with junk, keep it clear
Keep feeding your mind all your life through
It will give direction to all that you do
Don't be like the rest
Meet the test
Be your best.

Because life is tough you'll fail now and then
Pick yourself up and try again
Move past your failure, face the next thing

No failure is final for a child of the King
Don't be like the rest
Meet the test
Be your best.

Remember that many around you are down
Discouraged from being knocked around
They still have many challenges to meet
A kind word will get them back on their feet
Don't be like the rest
Meet the test
Be your best.

Excellence does not come to the man who alone
Tries to do everything on his own
Life is best when it is faced by a pair—
A person and God brought together in prayer
Don't be like the rest
Meet the test
Be your best.

No man is an island we have often been told
We need that message when life has us on hold
When the burdens of life get too heavy to bear
Remember the others with whom you can share
Don't be like the rest
Meet the test
Be your best.

God has made you to be your best
He's not satisfied with anything less
With your heart committed and your head bowed
Dare to rise above the crowd.
Don't be like the rest
Meet the test
Be your best.

NOTES

Chapter 1
1. *The Dallas Morning News*, 6 Apr. 1975.

Chapter 2
1. John W. Drakeford, *Wisdom for Today's Family* (Nashville: Broadman Press, 1978), pp. 24-25.
2. Numbers 13:30 (author's paraphrase).
3. Joshua 14:12, author's paraphrase.
4. Denis Waitley, *Seeds of Greatness* (Old Tappan, New Jersey: Fleming H. Revell Company, 1983), p. 36.
5. Carol Colman and Michael Perelman, *Late Bloomers* (New York: Ballantine Books, 1985), pp. 22-29.
6. *Newsweek*, Sept. 1972.
7. "Bits and Pieces," Vol. D/No. 2A, p. 18.

Chapter 3
1. Genesis 39:7 (author's paraphrase).
2. 2 Corinthians 12:7.
3. Genesis 45:5 (RSV).
4. Paul Aurandt, *More of Paul Harvey's the Rest of the Story* (New York: William Morrow and Co., 1980), pp. 141-42.
5. Robert H. Schuller, *You Can Become the Person You Want to Be* (New York: Hawthorn Books, 1973), pp. 15-16.
6. Genesis 39:7-9 (author's paraphrase).
7. *USA Today*, 24 Mar. 1987, p. 2c.
8. Waitley, p. 169.
9. Charles L. Wallis, ed., *Minister's Manual: 1982 Edition* (San Francisco: Harper and Row, 1982), p. 260.
10. E. Stanley Jones, *A Song of Ascents* (Nashville: Abingdon Press, 1968), p. 36.
11. Atlanta *Constitution*, July 20 1980, p. 2a.

Chapter 4
1. 2 Kings 6:8-23.
2. 2 Kings 6:15-16 (author's paraphrase).
3. 2 Kings 6:17 (NASB).
4. Schuller, p. 81.
5. Waitley, p. 189.

6. Moody Adams, *Conquest,* December, 1977.
7. Harry Emerson Fosdick, *What Is Vital in Religion?* (New York: Harper and Brothers, 1955), p. 2.
8. Wallis, p. 84.
9. Denis Waitley, *The Winner's Edge* (New York: Berkley Books, 1980), p. 97.
10. Mark H. McCormack, *What They Don't Teach You at Harvard Business School* (Toronto: Bantam Books, 1984), p. 53.

Chapter 5
1. Exodus 2:1-10.
2. *Pensacola Journal,* 1 Jan. 1979, p. 7a.
3. W. B. J. Martin, *Little Foxes that Spoil the Vines* (Nashville: Abingdon Press, 1968), p. 106.
4. Denis Waitley, *The Double Win* (Old Tappan, New Jersey: Fleming H. Revell Co., 1985), p. 118.
5. Cited by Raymond E. Jennison, "Freedom in Failure," *Pulpit Digest,* May-June 1983, p. 55.
6. Waitley, *Seeds of Greatness,* p. 76.
7. 1 John 4:18 (RSV).
8. *Quote,* Vol. 71, p. 272.
9. *Quote,* Vol. 77, p. 145.
10. *Quote,* Vol. 68, p. 469.

Chapter 6
1. Daniel 6:10 (NASB).
2. Og Mandino, *The Greatest Salesman in the World* (Toronto: Bantam Books, 1968), p. 54.
3. Donald E. Demaray, *Pulpit Giants: What Made Them Great* (Chicago: Moody Press, 1973), p. 55.
4. *Quote,* Vol. 82, p. 472.
5. W. Phillip Keller, *Wonder O' the Wind* (Waco: Word Books, 1982), p. 111.
6. William Barclay, *A Spiritual Autobiography* (Grand Rapids: Wm. B. Eerdmans, 1975), p. 112.
7. Robert J. Hastings, *My Money and God* (Nashville: Broadman Press, 1961), p. 16.
8. *Reader's Digest,* Apr. 1972, p. 24.
9. *Arkansas Gazette,* 6 May 1987, p. 5d.
10. Aurandt, p. 182.

Chapter 7
1. Philippians 3:13-14 (NASB).
2. Acts 6—7.
3. Philippians 3:13 (TLB).
4. Philippians 3:13-14(NASB).
5. Art Linklettr, *Hobo on the Way to Heaven* (Elgin, Ill.: David G. Cook Publishing Co., 1980), p. 193.
6. *Quote,* Vol. 69, p. 373.
7. *Quote,* Vol. 70, p. 218.
8. *Quote,* Vol. 69, p. 76.
9. *Reader's Digest,* Oct. 1971, p. 139.

Chapter 8
1. See Acts 18:24-28.

2. Acts 18:25-26 (NASB).

3. Fulton J. Sheen, *Treasure in Clay: The Autobiography of Fulton J. Sheen* (Garden City: Image Books, 1982), p. 300.

4. Philippians 4:8.

5. Harold E. Buell, "Is Your Bag Packed for Eternity?" *Pulpit Digest, Jan.-Feb. 1978,* p. 51.

6. *Quote,* Vol. 74, p. 83.

7. *The Dallas Morning News,* 25 Feb. 1977, p. 18a.

8. Cecil G. Osborne, *The Art of Getting Along with People* (Grand Rapids: Zondervan, 1980), p. 145.

9. Bryant M. Kirkland, "The Key Person in Your Life," *Pulpit Digest,* July-Aug. 1981, pp. 21-22.

10. Cited in Warren Wiersbe, *Be Joyful* (Wheaton: Ill. Victor Books, 1974), p. 116.

11. Proverbs 23:7 (NASB).

12. *Quote,* Vol. 71, p. 410.

13. 1 Corinthians 2:16.

14. 2 Corinthians 10:5 (NASB).

Chapter 9

1. Acts 4:36-37.

2. Acts 9:27.

3. Acts 11:23.

4. Acts 13:13.

5. Acts 15:37-39.

6. Waitley, *The Double Win,* pp. 86-87.

7. Paul Tournier, *Escape from Loneliness* (Philadelphia: The Westminster Press, 1962), p. 13.

8. Bruce Larson, *There's a Lot More to Health than Not Being Sick* (Waco: Word, 1981), p. 19.

9. Ralph W. Neighbour, Jr., and Cal Thomas, *Target-group Evangelism* (Nashville: Broadman Press, 1975), p. 62.

10. From the American Council of Life Insurance, cited in *Parade,* 10 Dec. 1978, p. 23.

11. Dr. Drew Gunnells, "God's Final Word," preached at Spring Hill Baptist Church, Mobile, Alabama, 11 Apr. 1982.

12. Nelson L. Price, *Supreme Happiness* (Nashville: Broadman Press, 1979), p. 108.

13. Gary R. Collins, *The Magnificent Mind* (Waco: Word Books, 1985), p. 208.

Chapter 10

1. Grant Teaff, *I Believe* (Waco: Word Books, 1975), pp. 152-54.

2. Acts 13:13.

3. Acts 15:39.

4. 2 Timothy 4:11.

5. Aurandt, pp. 118-21.

6. Ronald W. Clark, *Edison: The Man Who Made the Future* (New York: G. P. Putnam's Sons, 1977), p. 13.

7. Raymond W. Albright, *Focus on Infinity: A Life of Phillips Brooks* (New York: The Macmillan Co., 1961), pp. 29-31.

8. Clark, p. 71.

9. Alan Loy McGinnis, *Bringing Out the Best in People* (Minneapolis: Augsburg Publishing House, 1985), p. 72.

10. Larson, p. 92.

Chapter 11
1. Teaff, pp. 198-99.
2. Alexander Whyte, *Bible Characters* (Grand Rapids: Zondervan, 1967), p. 363.
3. Herbert Lockyer, *All the Men of the Bible* (Grand Rapids: Zondervan, 1958), p. 99.
4. J. Sidlow Baxter, *Explore the Book*, Vol. 2 (Grand Rapids: Zondervan, 1960), p. 111.
5. Ibid., p. 112.
6. 1 Kings 17:1.
7. 1 Kings, 17:2-7.
8. 1 Kings 17:10,24.
9. 1 Kings 18.
10. 1 Kings 19.
11. Luke 18:1.
12. James 4:2.
13. Philippians 4:19.
14. Schuller, p. 165.
15. Nathan Kline, *From Sad to Glad* (New York: G. P. Putnam's Sons, 1974), p. 9.
16. 1 Kings 19.
17. John 15:7 (NASB).
18. James 5:16 (NASB, author's italics).
19. Bruce Larson, *Dare to Live Now* (Grand Rapids: Zondervan, 1965), p.91.
20. Ephesians 2:18.
21. 1 Thessalonians 5:17.
22. 2 Kings 19:14.
23. John M. Drescher, "Empty Chair," *Pulpit Digest*, May-June 1981, p. 39.

Chapter 12
1. William Ernest Henley, "Invictus," ed. Ralph L. Woods, *A Treasury of the Familiar* (New York: The Macmillan Co., 1942), p. 97.
2. Exodus 18:13-22.
3. Exodus 17:8-16.
4. 1 Samuel 13:14.
5. 1 Samuel 18:7 (author's paraphrase).
6. 2 Samuel 23.
7. Maynard Campbell, "A Growing Faith for Changing Times," *Proclaim*, July-Sept. 1981, p. 15.
8. Alan Loy McGinnis, *The Friendship Factor* (Minneapolis: Augsburg Publishing House, 1979), p. 15.
9. James W. Cox, ed. *The Ministers Manual: 1984 Edition* (San Francisco: Harper and Row, 1984), p. 31.
10. Larry Christenson, *Back to Square One* (Minneapolis: The Bethany Fellowship, Inc., 1979), p. 77.
11. R. L. Middleton, *My Cup Runneth Over* (Nashville: Broadman Press, 1960), pp. 49-50.
12. Charles L. Wallis, ed., *Minister's Manual: 1979 Edition* (San Francisco: Harper and Row, 1979), p. 250.
13. McGinnis, pp. 20-81.
14. Ibid., p. 27.

Chapter 13
1. Ecclesiastes 9:10 (NASB).
2. 1 Corinthians 10:31 (NASB).
3. Waitley, *The Double Win*, p. 31.

4. Waitley, *The Winner's Edge*, p. 16.

5. Jack McCallum, "Doc Across America," *Sport's Illustrated*, 4 May 1987, p. 74.

6. Frank Deford, "A Star's Legacy," *Sport's Illustrated*, 4 May 1987, pp. 83-84.

7. Ibid., p. 84.